FIND YOUR PLACE IN GOD'S GREAT STORY

for Kids

PAUL BASDEN & JIM JOHNSON

HARVEST HOUSE PUBLISHERS
EUGENE, OREGON

Cover design by Dugan Design Group

Cover photo © tulaphn, artinspiring / Adobe Stock

Interior design by KUHN Design Group

Illustrations by Devon Laird

Finding Your Place in God's Great Story for Kids
Copyright © 2021 by Paul Basden and Jim Johnson
Published by Harvest House Publishers
Eugene, Oregon 97408
www.harvesthousepublishers.com

ISBN 978-0-7369-8123-1 (hardcover)
ISBN 978-0-7369-8124-8 (eBook)

Library of Congress Cataloging-in-Publication Data

Names: Basden, Paul, author. | Johnson, Jim (Pastor), author.
Title: Finding your place in God's great story for kids / Paul Basden and Jim Johnson.
Description: Eugene, Oregon : Harvest House Publishers, 2021. | Audience: Ages 9 to 12
Identifiers: LCCN 2020050334 (print) | LCCN 2020050335 (ebook) | ISBN 9780736981231 (hardcover) | ISBN 9780736981248 (ebook)
Subjects: LCSH: Bible—Introductions—Juvenile literature. | God (Christianity)—Biblical teaching—Juvenile literature. | Storytelling—Religious aspects—Christianity.
Classification: LCC BS539 .B37 2021 (print) | LCC BS539 (ebook) | DDC 220.6/1—dc23
LC record available at https://lccn.loc.gov/2020050334
LC ebook record available at https://lccn.loc.gov/2020050335

Printed in China

21 22 23 24 25 26 27 28 29 / RDS / 10 9 8 7 6 5 4 3 2 1

To three women who have inspired us most
to help children find their place in God's Great Story

Amy Mixon Marchino, Cindy Fiala, and Alison Leamon

Contents

The Power of Story

Star Wars.

The Avengers.

Harry Potter.

Indiana Jones.

The Lord of the Rings.

Other than making a ton of money, what do these film franchises have in common?

They all tell stories. Exciting stories. Thrilling stories. Compelling stories. Once you start watching, you can't stop. That's the power of a good story.

Story is all the rage these days. Authors, musicians, and screenwriters craft the best stories they can so we will read their books, listen to their songs, and watch their movies. There are even experts who use stories to sell things, from toothbrushes to TVs to Toyotas. The power of story is visible everywhere.

But story is not just something you read on a page or watch in a theater. Story is also something you live. *You* have a story. Everyone you know has a story. Even God has a story—a Great Story. This book is about God's Great Story, and it's about your story too.

GOD HAS A STORY

How do you make friends with another person? You may meet them at the lunch table on your first day of school, or share a desk with them in class, or play on the same soccer team. You might ask them a question about something you notice, like the type of sandwich they are eating, and then they ask you a question. Before long, you start to understand who they are. You know their story. When you know someone's story, you know *them*. When they know your story, they know *you*.

This is true about God too. If you were to meet God face to face, you might ask him, "Could you tell me about yourself?" God might reply, "Have a seat and kick up your feet—it's going to take a while. Are you ready? Here goes..." The story he would tell you can be found in only one place.

God's Story Is Told in the Bible

When you hear the word "Bible," do you yawn? Do you think of it as a list of rules to obey or a bunch of boring old stories?

Ugh!

We want to let you in on a secret: There is an incredible, interesting, powerful story in the Bible, just waiting for you to discover it. The Bible tells God's Great Story.

And it is epic.

The Creator creating this world at the sound of a word. The world falling into darkness because of human sin and evil. God redeeming it all, bringing the world back to himself and making it perfect. It's all in God's Great Story.

It's a tale that stretches from creation to re-creation, from Genesis to Revelation, from beginning to end and beyond—on to a new beginning that will *never* end.

Here is God's Great Story in a nutshell: God created a world of humans he could know and love, and though they got lost in stubbornness and rebellion, he brought them back to himself through his own sacrificial love.

All the other stories in the Bible point toward that Great Story.

God's Story Has Eight Great Chapters

The Bible is filled with hundreds of stories. You can read about Adam and Eve, Abraham and Sarah, Moses and Joshua, David and Goliath, Elijah and Elisha, Ruth and Esther. And that's just the Old Testament! In the New Testament we encounter Mary and Joseph, Jesus and the Twelve, Peter and John, Herod and Pilate, Paul and Barnabas...and the list goes on.

The Bible is a *great* story. So we are telling God's Great Story in just eight chapters. We will share with you the greatest of the great ideas in the biblical story. Each chapter also focuses on an important character, someone God uses to move his Great Story forward.

These eight chapters tell God's Story. They go like this:

1. God Creates (Adam and Eve)

2. God Blesses (Abraham)

3. God Rescues (Moses)

4. God Chooses (David)

5. God Warns (the prophets)

6. God Saves (Jesus)

7. God Sends (Paul)

8. God Wins (John)

FINDING YOUR PLACE
IN GOD'S GREAT STORY

Do you ever lie in bed at night and ask, "What is happening? Why is my story taking all these twists and turns?" You may think about today's bloopers, yesterday's blow-ups, or last year's blunders. You want to make sense of it all.

If you want more answers, it will help to look beyond your own life and experiences. Together, we will learn to look at your story in light of God's Story, which is the only way your story will ever make sense! Believe it or not, God has an exciting part for you to play in his story! He wants you to see it too. And look forward to it. And embrace it.

So have a seat and listen up. God is about to tell you his Great Story. You're about to find your place in it. Could anything be better?

1

God Creates

Before there is space or time or anything else at all, there is God. Majestic and mysterious. All in all. Nothing besides him. Everything and the Only Thing.

From this place, before time and space (and rhymes) exist, God decides to create the world! The Ultimate Designer fills the world with incredible, awesome things. He also decides to create humans to live in that world.

He will make humans to be like himself. They will think! Feel! Create! They will make big, important decisions! Humans, like God, will be free. Able to say yes or no—even to God—however they choose.

So God starts creating.

And BANG! Galaxies whirl into place, oceans fill the deep spaces, and living creatures appear, all at the sound of a word from God.

He takes a special interest in humans. He gives them gifts and abilities to help take care of his whole creation.

CREATION AND GENESIS 1

"Wait," you may be thinking, "God said a *word*, and everything showed up, just like that? Did it all happen right away? Did it take millions of years? I've heard different things from different people, and I need a straight answer."

We get it. You may have big questions about how creation happened. Did it take seven days or forever and a day? What about dinosaurs? Can God make a rock so big even he can't lift it? No, really, *what about dinosaurs*?

God gave you a curious mind for a reason, and it's good to ask questions like those! The *way* God created the world is a question about *how*. Right now, though, we have a big question of our own we want to talk about, and it's maybe the greatest question of all: *Why*?

Why did God do all of this, and what does his Great Story tell us about him?

We want to talk about God's Great Story. And as you probably know, the best place to begin is IN THE BEGINNING. (Feel free to read that in a big, booming voice.)

So in a spirit of discovery and curiosity, check out the opening chapters in the Bible, in the book of Genesis.

HOW TO READ GENESIS 1

Since the words in Genesis were written a long time ago, reading them is not the same as reading a story that just came out yesterday. But don't worry, we're here to help you out. Here are a few things to keep in mind.

Genesis 1 Is Prehistoric

That's right, prehistoric. Okay, now that you're finished imagining a triceratops fighting a tyrannosaurus rex, or a snaggletoothed caveman hunting a saber-toothed tiger, let's get started. "Prehistoric" means that the things Genesis 1 talks about happened before anyone knew how to write things down.

We know that the call of Abraham, whom you'll meet soon, happened around 2,000 BC, but Genesis 1 goes back to the earliest moments of cosmic history, way before Abraham (or anyone else) was alive.

That means nobody was around to put the story on their social media timeline. There wasn't even such a thing yet as time!

So what happened?

We believe that God created the heavens and the earth. We also believe that God inspired people later on to write down what happened. Everything that happened before people wrote things down? That's "prehistoric." That's where we find the story of creation.

Genesis 1 Is Prescientific

When God inspired the ancient Hebrews (you'll meet them soon too) to write Genesis 1, he didn't pull them aside and whisper, "Pssst, while you're at it, be sure to say the earth is round like a ball, and it goes around the sun."

The ancient people who wrote the first part of God's Great Story didn't have that information. They thought that the earth was flat and that the sun went around the earth. But God was still able to tell his story through them.

If your mind likes to work on *how* questions, that's amazing! Science is really good at answering *how* questions. (And those answers go a long way toward making our lives better. Yay, science!)

But remember, we want to know more about *why*. And that's where God's Great Story has something to tell everyone!

Genesis 1 Is Theological

"Theology" is a big word that means "the study of God." That's what Genesis 1 is—a study of God. It tells us about a God who created a world full of wonders, including human beings.

It's the story of a world where people are designed to be connected with God, with each other, and with all of creation.

Genesis 1 is not about *how* and *when* the world was created, but about *who* created it and *why*. Focusing only on *how* and *when* things were created can make you miss what God is trying to say to you about himself.

But if you look for the *who* and the *why*, you'll be a real student of God!

 ## THE MAIN CHARACTER IS GOD

"In the beginning God created the heavens and the earth" (Genesis 1:1).

You will meet many characters in Genesis, but the main character in the creation story is…(drumroll, please)…the Creator!

 ## GOD CREATED EVERYTHING

The author of Genesis 1 spreads the story of creation over seven days. In Hebrew, the word for "day" is *yom*, and it can mean a literal day (as in, there are 24 hours in a *yom*, there are 7 *yoms* in a week, and so on). But it doesn't only mean a 24-hour period of time; *yom* can also mean a time somewhere in the future.

For example, you might say to yourself, "One *day* I will be taller than my dad!" or "I'm going to be a professional acrobat one *day*!" That doesn't mean you'll become a six-foot-tall trapeze artist by this time tomorrow, does it? (No, unfortunately not.)

We believe that when "day" is used in Genesis 1–2, it means however long it took for God to create the heavens and the earth.

What's most important is this: God created it all. Whether he created the universe in an instant or over a long period of time, God is still the Creator.

Now let's look at each of the days of creation. Days one, two, and three describe three parts of the cosmic reality God created: time, space, and earth.

Day One: Time

> Then God said, "Let there be light," and there was light. And God saw that the light was good. Then he separated the light from the darkness. God called the light "day" and the darkness "night."
>
> And evening passed and morning came, marking the first day (Genesis 1:3-5).

Before God created this world, there was no such thing as time. But once day and night entered the picture, time became something we can be aware of and measure.

Time is the progression of events as we experience them. We measure it by what is happening now (the present), what happened before (the past), and what is going to happen (the future).

We can measure time in big chunks like years, decades, and centuries (that's 100 years). We can measure it in tiny bits, like seconds and minutes. But usually we measure time in days. We ask ourselves, "What are we going to do today?" We count the number of days till summer break. The day you learned to ride a bike was a big day.

Day one in God's Great Story is all about time.

Day Two: Space

> Then God said, "Let there be a space between the waters, to separate the waters of the heavens from the waters of the earth." And that is what happened. God made this space to separate the waters of the earth from the waters of the heavens. God called the space "sky."
>
> And evening passed and morning came, marking the second day (Genesis 1:6-8).

"Space" here means the sky directly over our heads, outer space waayyy above us, and "deep space" astronomically beyond us. (Cue the *Star Trek* theme song.)

Day Three: the Earth

> Then God said, "Let the waters beneath the sky flow together into one place, so dry ground may appear." And that is what happened. God called the dry ground "land" and the waters "seas." And God saw that it was good. Then God said, "Let the

land sprout with vegetation..." And that is what happened...
And God saw that it was good.

And evening passed and morning came, marking the third
day (Genesis 1:9-13).

Earth includes plants, trees, and fruits that are given to nourish us, and
the soil in which they grow.

Days Four, Five, and Six

In the first three days of creation found in Genesis 1, we see God creating time, space, and the earth. On the next three days, God assigns a
ruler over each of those things.

On day four, God brings out the sun to rule the day and the moon to
rule the night. This is how we measure time.

Birds and fish show up on day five to make the most of God's work on
day two—the sky and the sea. The birds rule the air above us, and the
fish rule the sea below.

On day six, God creates animals and humans, connecting us back to the
original Earth Day (day three). The humans and animals on day six are
called to rule over and take care of the earth.

 GOD RESTED

The chapter ends with day seven. That's when God rested.

> So the creation of the heavens and the earth and everything in them was completed. On the seventh day God had finished his work of creation, so he rested from all his work. And God blessed the seventh day and declared it holy, because it was the day when he rested from all his work of creation (Genesis 2:1-3).

Was God so tired from creating an entire universe that he had to take a heavenly power nap? Not quite.

God wasn't even close to being tired. Instead, he took time to look at what he had made and *enjoyed* it! He celebrated creation! Everything in its right place. Everything in order. Everything humming along just like he intended. This is what God celebrated when he looked at all he had done.

GOD CREATED HUMANS

Hold up! Wait a minute! We skipped over something on day six that is pretty important. Let's go back.

> Then God said, "Let us make human beings in our image, to be like us. They will reign over the fish in the sea, the birds in the sky, the livestock, all the wild animals on the earth, and the small animals that scurry along the ground."

> So God created human beings in his own image.
>> In the image of God he created them;
>>> male and female he created them

> Then God blessed them and said, "Be fruitful and multiply. Fill the earth and govern it. Reign over the fish in the sea, the birds in the sky, and all the animals that scurry along the ground" (Genesis 1:26-28).

Humans are made to be like God. This is a revolutionary teaching: Human creatures are created to be like their Creator! (Seriously, no one else was saying this when Genesis 1 was written. It was a pretty big deal.)

Being created in the image of God means that our minds, emotions, and wills reflect the thinking, feeling, and willing of God. We represent God as his corulers and cocreators over all the earth. But more than anything, we are designed to connect meaningfully to God and to others.

Whew! What an eventful week! So much good work done! But God sees that something isn't quite right. What could it be? Let's take a look.

GOD CREATED MARRIAGE

> Then the LORD God said, "It is not good for the man to be alone. I will make a helper who is just right for him…"

> So the LORD God caused the man to fall into a deep sleep. While the man slept, the LORD God took out one of the man's

ribs and closed up the opening. Then the LORD God made a woman from the rib, and he brought her to the man.

"At last!" the man exclaimed.

> "This one is bone from my bone,
>   and flesh from my flesh!
> She will be called 'woman,'
>   because she was taken from 'man.'"

This explains why a man leaves his father and mother and is joined to his wife, and the two are united into one (Genesis 2:18,21-24).

When God looks at the man, he exclaims, "Wait a minute...you still look lonely to me!"

So God gave us marriage as a gift to help fix the problem of being alone. That doesn't mean you have to get married someday if you don't want to. (Jesus never got married, and he had the fullest life there is!) But it was a great idea of God's to give us the choice.

WHAT CREATION MEANS TO YOU

When you think about the Creator, creation, or creating, what do you think of? Do you imagine a room full of art supplies—colorful paint pots, brushes, markers, pens, and pencils? Do you see yourself doing something cool that no one else can do, like landing a skateboard trick or solving a difficult math problem? Or do you think about the wonders of nature, the beauty of the outdoors, where you can see things growing and being re-created all around you?

You are created to be a creator! This is a chance for you to put your own God-given abilities to use. What do you want to create in the world? What do you feel like making or doing right now? So what are you waiting for? Get to creating!

Creation Is a Gift

You may have gotten this far and already started to ask our big question yourself: Why?

Why did God make the world? Why did he make people? Why did he make you? He didn't have to do it. He wasn't missing anything—he's perfect! So why did he do anything at all?

God created because he wanted to.

Why did he want to create?

Because God is love. It's that simple.

God was so filled with love that he decided to create humans in order to have someone else to love. Loving others for no other reason than just to do it—that's what we call grace. And that's a large part of understanding the *why* of God's Great Story.

Creation Is Good

God called his creation good, and in the case of us humans, very good. (Not to brag.)

What God first made was wonderful, but sin and evil have made some things in God's creation ugly. We've sure messed up a lot! But whenever you experience the ugliness we sometimes make of it, keep in mind that God's original creation is still beautiful.

Creation Is Purposeful

It doesn't say so in Genesis 1–2, but when God's Great Story gets to the New Testament, it's clear: Creation is all about Jesus. Here's what the New Testament says:

> Christ is the visible image of the invisible God.
> He existed before anything was created
> and is supreme over all creation,
> for through him God created everything
> in the heavenly realms and on earth.
> He made the things we can see
> and the things we can't see—
> such as thrones, kingdoms, rulers,
> and authorities in the unseen world.
> Everything was created through him and for him
> (Colossians 1:15-16).

Spoiler alert: Chapter 8 is where you'll find out how God the Father finally gives to Jesus the Son all that has ever been created. But don't read ahead. (Trust us, it's worth the wait.)

THE REST OF THE STORY

The Story Goes Wrong

Creation is chapter 1 in God's Great Story. Things are off to a great start! The sun and moon are brand-new, fish are swimming, birds are singing, and humans are about to begin a great adventure as cocreators with the Ultimate Creator.

Then it all goes wrong.

What happens? Adam and Eve decide that being *like* God isn't good enough. They want to *be* God themselves. They want to know everything God knows. They choose to say no to God.

It does not go well. Sin enters the world. God's image in humans becomes disfigured. Moms and dads struggle. Family members kill each other. Nations go to war. Paradise seems lost.

But that's not the end of the story.

God Doesn't Give Up

Even though humans turned against God, he doesn't give up on them. He has a purpose for creation and will follow through on it, whatever it takes.

It's one thing to say you *believe* in God's Great Story. It's a totally different thing to say you *belong* in God's Story.

But you do. We all do.

At the end of Genesis 1, we discover our big job as humans in God's creation.

> Then God blessed them and said, "Be fruitful and multiply. Fill the earth and govern it. Reign over the fish in the sea, the birds in the sky, and all the animals that scurry along the ground" (Genesis 1:28).

We are made to rule wisely over God's creation. Here's what that means.

YOU ARE GOD'S APPRENTICE

God is the great "capital C" Creator, and he chose you to be one of his junior creators. You're a part of the family business of creating. God wants you to use your intellect and imagination. He invites you to create (and improve!) the way the world works—the way we grow food; the way we make, buy, sell, and trade things; the art and music we make;

the technology we use; even how you choose to spend your free time. God's vision for your creativity is endless! He wants you to help make the world more like he intended it to be. You are his apprentice.

 ## YOU ARE GOD'S MANAGER

We don't just get to create; God also gives us responsibility over things that he already made. This means we must be wise and considerate when it comes to protecting nature. The earth God created depends on humans to tend to it and bring the best out of it. It is also incredibly precious—to our knowledge, God only made this one! We need to help it last so people in the future can enjoy it as well.

 ## YOU ARE GOD'S REPRESENTATIVE

A representative is someone who officially acts on behalf of one group to another. That means God has appointed you to represent him in the world. He has put you on earth to mirror to others who he really is and to love the people he loves (which is everyone!). It's a big job, so you might not know where to start.

Here is a chance for you to be creative. Take some time and think about how you can be God's representative in your family, at school, in your neighborhood, and in the world. Then write it down or draw a picture of one action you can take and put it somewhere you can see it. This will be a daily reminder of how to represent God in your own way!

God the Creator has written you into his story of creation. You have important roles to play as an apprentice, a manager, and a representative. It's what you were made for!

JUST THE BEGINNING

God's grace toward sinful humans is just the beginning of his Great Story. It's an incredible story of a God who...

- Blesses the world by beginning a new nation and calling them his chosen people, starting with just an old shepherd and his wife

- Rescues his people from slavery and delivers them to the Land of Promise

- Chooses a young man "after God's heart" to lead his people

- Warns his people through prophets (professional truth-tellers) that they must reject idolatry and injustice if they are to be his people

- Saves the world through a Jewish carpenter who is also the Son of God

- Sends the Good News out into the world through a rabbi turned apostle

- Wins the final victory over sin, evil, and death and brings into existence a new heaven and new earth

Buckle up, gang! This will be quite a ride.

The Story Between the Story

After Adam and Eve are banished from the Garden, they have Cain and Abel. The first recorded case of sibling rivalry happens when God accepts Abel's offering but rejects Cain's. It gets intense. Cain kills Abel, is banished from his family, settles east of Eden, marries, has a son he names Enoch and founds a city he names... Enoch. (Cain may have been a great farmer, but apparently, he was not a creative thinker.)

As more and more people fill the earth, mankind becomes increasingly wicked. God is sorry he ever created humans, and his heart is broken. In all the earth, only Noah is righteous, so God instructs him to build a huge boat to save the animals and his family from a catastrophic flood. After the waters recede, Noah builds an altar to offer sacrifices to God, and God gives a rainbow as a sign of his covenant to never again destroy all living things with a flood.

God blesses Noah and his sons Shem, Ham, and Japheth, commanding them to be fruitful and multiply. Soon the earth is populous, everyone speaks the same language, and they think they're the coolest thing since sliced bread (which has not yet been invented). To display their general awesomeness to the world, the people build a great city with a tower reaching to the sky. God says, "Yeah, no" and confuses their language so they stop building and scatter.

One of Noah's sons, Shem, has a particularly important lineage. Shem has Arphaxad, who has Shelah, who has Eber, who has Peleg, who has Reu, who has Serug, who has Nahor, who has Terah, who has Abram, who lives in the land of Ur.

Abram marries a woman named Sarai. His father, Terah, takes Abram, Sarai, and Abram's nephew, Lot, and heads from Ur toward Canaan. But they stop and settle in Haran.

And that, in a nutshell, is the story between the story.

HARAN

CANAAN

UR

Abram

Sarai

Isaac

2nd

Cain

1st

Abel

2

God Blesses

Several years into the family adventure in Haran, the Lord comes to Abram, now 75, which is old even for Bible times. God makes him an incredible offer—picturesque land, thousands of descendants (kids and grandkids and great-grandkids and so on), and a chance to be remembered for a long time (several thousand years and counting!). There's just one catch: Abram will have to give up most everything he has—his home, his father's family, and his lifelong friends. Throwing caution to the wind, Abram packs up his belongings, says goodbye, and is off on a new adventure.

The key to God's promise is the birth of a son for Abram and Sarai. The trouble is, Sarai is old enough to be a grandmother, except she never had any kids of her own. Call them crazy (or crazy old!), but Abram and Sarai trusted that God would make good on his promise. They just had no idea it would take him another...wait for it...25 years!

Meanwhile, God decides to give Abram and Sarai new names—Abraham and Sarah. In Hebrew, Abram means "Father," while Abraham means "Father of Many." Sarai means "whiny and quarrelsome," but Sarah means "princess." That is a solid name upgrade for sure!

The time finally arrives, and the Lord shows up with a small entourage of angels to tell Abraham that Sarah is going to have a baby soon. Sarah, now ninety, overhears their conversation and bursts out laughing right in front of God and everybody. Awkward!

The Lord decides Abraham and Sarah should name the baby Isaac, which means...you guessed it...laughter.

Abraham turns one hundred, Isaac is born, and God's promise is up and running. Isaac will have two sons named Jacob and Esau. Jacob will have twelve sons who become the twelve tribes of Israel.

> You can read the official version of God's blessing to Abraham in Genesis chapters 12–25.

GOD'S STORY

God's Story is not a monologue (like in a play or movie where one character talks and talks and talks, and no one else gets to say anything). Since God created humans to be cocreators, he invites other characters onto the stage to help tell the Story, move the action along, and reveal his gracious nature and purpose for creation. God's interaction with Abraham pulls back the curtain to show who God is, what he is up to, who we are, and why we are here. Want to find out what is behind that curtain? Great! Let's explore God's role in this chapter of his Great Story.

God's own story doesn't really have a beginning (that's part of what makes him God—he's been around literally forever), but God's calling of Abraham represents a fresh start in *our* story.

You remember from chapter 1 how Adam and Eve start off with a bang but don't finish well? Their refusal to trust God has big, big consequences. After Adam and Eve mess up, generation after generation of these freshly minted humans turn away from their Creator. And they turn hard. God's heart is broken by their rejection. He is even sorry he came up with this big idea in the first place. (Check out Genesis 6:6.)

It gets so bad that God is ready to hit the reset button. This is where Noah shows up in the story as the only true friend God has left. Noah gets a heads-up from God about some extreme climate change and receives blueprints for a floating zoo. When Noah has all the animals on board and the unsinkable circus is ready to set sail, God shakes the Etch-a-Sketch of humanity and wipes everyone out with a huge storm—all except Noah and his family. People talk a lot about Noah's ark, because wow, what a big boat. But it turns out that what is most important is that one of his sons, Shem, is going to be the great-great-great-great-great-great-great-grandfather of Abraham.

God reboots his relationship with human beings when he invites Abraham to partner up with him to tell the biggest story ever. God and Abraham make a covenant (a.k.a. a "deal") with each other. A covenant is an agreement that transforms two or more groups or two or more people into one brand-new thing.

This new covenant transforms Abraham's life and helps us to understand the rest of God's Great Story. It's kind of similar to the way putting a picture in a frame helps you to see the image better.

God and Abraham's relationship takes thirteen chapters of Genesis to cover, but it's the invitation to the deal that reveals the hope and heart of God. Here's how Genesis records it:

> The LORD had said to Abram, "Leave your native country, your relatives, and your father's family, and go to the land that I will show you. I will make you into a great nation. I will bless you and make you famous, and you will be a blessing to others. I will bless those who bless you and curse those who treat you with contempt. All the families on earth will be blessed through you" (Genesis 12:1-3).

These three short verses kick off the story of God's redeeming work in and through the nation of Israel. From the establishment of this covenant, the plotlines (big ideas that hold a story together) of God's Great Story begin to flow. Some, if not all, of these plotlines will appear in every chapter of God's Great Story, creating the profound tapestry (a big picture made out of individual threads woven together) of mankind's living history with God. Here are the threads to watch out for.

GOD'S PURPOSE

It's safe to say God doesn't do things by accident. He always does things on purpose. Reaching out to Abraham was God's intentional effort to create a community of people he could love and call his own. God wants a deep, meaningful relationship with his creation. That's why throughout the Old and New Testaments, God says things like this: "You will be my people, and I will be your God." That idea shows up fifty-one times in the Bible, beginning in Genesis 17:7, when God speaks to Abraham, and ending in Revelation 21:3, where John envisions God making all things new at the end of time. John writes, "God's home is now among his people! He will live with them, and they will be his people. God himself will be with them."

God calls to Abraham. He's inviting him to become the proud parent of a new people who will live in life-giving fellowship with God. And it's not meant to be a small, cozy, "only cool kids get to hang out with us" kind of family. It's to be a God-sized community that incorporates all people everywhere into one gigantic family. As you continue to read God's Great Story, you'll notice this invitation comes up a lot.

GOD'S BLESSING

If God is seeking to create a people to love and call his own, it makes total sense that he would give them his favor and blessing.

The words "bless" and "blessing" pop up five times in just two verses as God talks to Abraham (Genesis 12:2-3). Not only that, there are over 600 mentions of it in the Old Testament alone. We are just getting started in God's Great Story, and it is already becoming clear that God is downright serious about blessing people!

He's so serious in fact, that as part of Abraham's agreement, God promises not only to bless Abraham but also to bless *all* the families on earth!

Ever hear someone say we are "blessed to be a blessing?" (If not, you have now!) This part of God's Story is where that idea gets started.

In the New Testament chapters of God's Great Story, you'll hear Jesus say things like these: "Give as freely as you have received." "Just as I have loved you, you should love each other." You'll hear Paul, one of the first people to tell the world about Jesus, say, "Be kind to each other, tenderhearted, forgiving one another, just as God through Christ has forgiven you" (Matthew 10:8; John 13:34; Ephesians 4:32). God likes to bless others, and he wants us to experience what it feels like to give blessings too. That's why he makes "paying it forward" part of every invitation he sends out to individuals in his Story.

 GOD'S INVITATION

Do you want to learn a lot about other people? Watch the way they make new friends and also how they treat the ones they have. Do they play nice? Do they share? Or do they yell and shout and always have to have their way?

God could make new friends any way he wanted to, and there would be nothing anyone could do about it. He could program people to be like NPCs (that's non-playable characters, if your parents are asking) in video games, making everyone on earth (including you) think, say, and do everything just the way he wants them to. That might be fun for a while, but it gets old fast.

What's more fun, playing the same one-player game over and over again with no one but the preprogramed characters to talk to, or playing co-op mode (your parents may look confused, so explain to them what that is, please) with a team of people who can think for themselves, capable of saying and doing surprising and amazing things?

God understands that true loving relationships happen only when everyone has the freedom to love—or not. That's why when he reaches out to humans to be in a relationship with him, his offer always comes as an invitation. No threats. No arm-twisting. No pushing, shoving, or yelling. Just a personal invitation, addressed specifically to you. You can reply yes, no, or maybe.

But don't answer before giving it some serious thought. This is not an invite to a regular old party. There are no presents or cake. There's no weird guy dressed up like Spider-Man making balloon animals (thank goodness!).

Saying yes to God's invitation means you are accepting a difficult challenge, turning your personal story with a lowercase "s" into something greater. You'll be joining a Story, one worth telling again and again and again.

ABRAHAM'S RESPONSE

Abraham says yes to God's big, challenging invitation. He packs up his tents and toys. He asks his wife and favorite nephew to do the same, and together they head off to their new home. Here is how Genesis records it:

> So Abram departed as the LORD had instructed, and Lot went with him. Abram was seventy-five years old when he left Haran. He took his wife, Sarai, his nephew Lot, and all his wealth—his livestock and all the people he had taken into his household at Haran—and headed for the land of Canaan. When they arrived in Canaan, Abram traveled through the land as far as Shechem. There he set up camp beside the oak of Moreh. At that time, the area was inhabited by Canaanites.
>
> Then the LORD appeared to Abram and said, "I will give this land to your descendants." And Abram built an altar there and dedicated it to the LORD, who had appeared to him (Genesis 12:4-7).

Abraham's decision shows what the word "trust" really means. Are you wondering why we are using the word "trust" and not another word, like "faith"? Good question! Here's why.

You know that a noun is a person, place, or thing, and that verbs are action words, right?

Remember, the Bible wasn't written in English at first. In the original Bible languages, "faith" was both a thing (noun) and an action (verb). In English, though, "faith" is only a noun. It doesn't make sense to say "Abraham faithed in God," does it?

In English, "trust" is a noun *and* a verb. Abraham makes an active response to God's promise. Abraham has a belief (noun) about God's power to make his promise a reality, and he is willing to reorder (verb) his whole life around what he believes to be true.

He doesn't just believe that God *can* fulfill the promise; he trusts that he *will*. Abraham doesn't just let the story happen to him; he takes an active part in God's Great Story. So Abraham packs up the U-Haul and heads west. (Because he did that, over a thousand years later in God's Great Story, two New Testament writers remember Abraham and talk about him as a hero of faith! But we're getting way ahead of ourselves.)

Abraham's trust in God's promise does not go unrewarded. God comes through on everything he said he would do. Abraham becomes one of the most influential people in history. The three largest monotheistic religions ("mono" means "one," and "theistic" means "God")—Judaism, Christianity, and Islam—all can be traced to him.

This man who had zero kids by the time he turned 100 now has four billion people who call him "father Abraham." Which brings us to the last plotline.

GOD'S CHARACTER

Even though Abraham and Sarah have *huge* doubts (and way to go for noticing that even faithful people have doubts!), God demonstrates his character by being faithful to the end. He doesn't do things immediately, or whenever Abraham thinks would be best, but God still comes through on his promise in ways Abraham could never have imagined.

> The LORD kept his word and did for Sarah exactly what he had promised. She became pregnant, and she gave birth to a son for Abraham in his old age. This happened at just the time God had said it would. And Abraham named their son Isaac. Eight days after Isaac was born, Abraham circumcised him as God had commanded. Abraham was 100 years old when Isaac was born.
>
> And Sarah declared, "God has brought me laughter. All who hear about this will laugh with me. Who would have said to Abraham that Sarah would nurse a baby? Yet I have given Abraham a son in his old age!" (Genesis 21:1-7).

As God's Story reveals, his faithfulness is not a limited resource. Through every generation, he makes his faithfulness known by rescuing, forgiving, renewing, and restoring his people again and again. And here's more good news: You are included in the story too!

We love stories. We identify with particular characters—they draw us in, and we feel what they feel. One part of Abraham's and Sarah's story we haven't talked about yet might actually be where you connect the most with God's Great Story. Before they were involved in God's Great Story, Abraham and Sarah felt...empty.

THE FEELING OF EMPTINESS

Sarah could not have children, and everybody knew it. She felt ashamed because she didn't have something she felt like everyone else had or was supposed to have. She felt like something was wrong with her and no one else could understand. She felt empty.

It wasn't much better for Abraham. Not having children with Sarah meant no one would carry on his name after he was gone. Emptiness hung over him and Sarah, following them wherever they went.

Abraham's spirit was also empty. He grew up in a family that believed there were many gods—gods of rocks and trees, gods of the neighborhood he lived in, even gods that were just around because his parents and grandparents worshipped them.

These gods that people used to believe in didn't care much for people. In fact, people thought that if you didn't keep them happy, they would seriously mess up your day. People decided the best way to keep the gods from flattening them with a rock, or whatever else they were afraid of, was to offer sacrifices to them.

But how could you know if you had sacrificed enough to keep from getting squished? Were two pigeons enough? Did you need to sacrifice a lamb or a calf? If you're not getting the results you want, sacrifice more! No price is too high to keep the gods from chucking a big ol' boulder right at your noggin.

Some people were so scared of making the gods angry, they even sacrificed their own kids. (Yikes!)

It is in this extreme emptiness of body and soul that God finds Abraham and offers him hope.

GOD SPEAKS HOPE

Perhaps, like Abraham and Sarah, you feel empty. There may be times when the world looks dry and dirty, even on a sunny day. You might see people who look like there isn't a single thing wrong in their lives, and you might feel mad that your life doesn't look the same.

Emptiness can infect any part of our lives. Whenever and wherever we feel alone, emptiness is right there, making us feel worse. Thankfully, God has included us in his promise to Abraham!

Toward the end of God's Great Story you'll learn more about the apostle Paul, who was just mentioned earlier. He writes a letter to a group of Jesus-followers who feel alone in their own city, a place called Galatia. He encourages them like this:

> In the same way, "Abraham believed God, and God counted him as righteous because of his faith." The real children of Abraham, then, are those who put their faith in God.
>
> What's more, the Scriptures looked forward to this time when God would make the Gentiles right in his sight because of their faith. God proclaimed this good news to Abraham long ago when he said, "All nations will be blessed through you." So all who put their faith in Christ share the same blessing Abraham received because of his faith (Galatians 3:6-9).

This is incredible news! Just like God reached out to Abraham, he is reaching out to you too! In Christ, God promises you a truly radical future. Even if you feel like your story is trapped in the land of emptiness, God can write a new chapter in your life. All he requires from you is what he required of Abraham—trust!

It's early in the story, and there is still so much to discover about God. It might be too early to ask you to believe 100 percent in his promise so close to the beginning of the story.

But do us a favor, will you please? As you learn more of God's Story, pay close attention to how often he is faithful to people. God's faithfulness does not expire or go bad. There is no limit to how many times he will show up and follow up on his promise to his people.

The Story Between the Story

When Abraham's son Isaac grows up, Abraham wants to find him a wife. Enter Rebekah, who shows us that it always pays to water a man's camels. Isaac and Rebekah have twins—Esau and Jacob (think cats and dogs). Jacob steals Esau's birthright and blessing, skips town, and dreams of a stairway to heaven (minus the guitar solo). He falls in love with the beautiful Rachel but gets tricked into first marrying her sister Leah, who...well, let's just say she has a great personality. Jacob and Esau reconcile, and then Jacob wrestles with God (literally) and gets a new name: Israel. (Don't be confused. The nation was named after him and came later.) He has a whole bunch of kids but plays favorites and gives Joseph an awesome coat. Joseph is a dreamer and a bit of a smarty-pants, so his brothers decide to teach him a lesson by selling him into slavery in Egypt and telling their father he's dead. (And you think you've got sibling problems!)

God is with Joseph, and he earns his Egyptian master's favor, but then he's sent to prison for something he didn't do. After years in prison, he interprets Pharaoh's crazy dream and goes from prison to the palace as Pharaoh's right-hand man. A famine forces Joseph's brothers to search for food in Egypt, and when they arrive they eat like kings. What they don't know is that the man they bow before is the king's right-hand man. He's also their long-lost brother, whom they don't recognize. Joseph cries tears of joy, forgives his brothers, and is reunited with his father, and the whole family is invited to come and live like royalty in Egypt.

After Jacob dies, the brothers are afraid that Joseph will use the opportunity to finally get revenge on them. Much to their surprise, Joseph tells them something so profound that not only are they relieved of their fears, but all these years later it is still worth retweeting—"You intended to harm me, but God intended it all for good" (Genesis 50:20).

For hundreds of years, the children of Israel live and prosper and multiply in the land of Egypt.

And that, in a nutshell, is the story between the story.

3

God Rescues

It is a dark chapter in God's Great Story. Pharaoh enslaves the descendants of Abraham (the Israelites) in Egypt, far from the Promised Land of Canaan. From this most unlikely place, a hero rises—Moses, Israel's first and greatest prophet. Born a slave, raised in a royal palace to a life of privilege, and then banished from his home for forty years, Moses encounters the God of his ancestors in the desert wastes. Charged by God to free his people from slavery, Moses leads the Israelites out of Egypt and into the Land of Promise!

You can read the full story of God rescuing Israel from Egypt in Exodus 1–19.

God's Story always gives us a hero to root for. God picks Abraham to start a new nation called Israel. But years and years later, when God's people wind up in Egypt instead of in the Promised Land, God chooses a new leader to get them back on track. Enter Moses.

GOD RESCUES MOSES

At a certain point in every good story, someone gets in trouble and needs to be rescued. It happens again and again in the Bible, so you'll also see it a lot in this book. In chapter 3 of God's Great Story, the pattern goes like this: God rescues Moses so that Moses can rescue Israel so that Israel can rescue the world. Why do God's people need rescuing? Great question! Let's start there!

God's People Suffer

God promised Abraham, his son Isaac, and his grandson Jacob the land of Canaan as their permanent home. Then a famine comes along, and Jacob's whole family heads to Egypt in search of food. They travel all the way to a place in the Nile Delta called Goshen. Abraham's great-grandson Joseph is Pharaoh's right-hand man, so the Israelites have all the food they need. And the Israelites live happily ever after. Until...

It's four hundred years later, and things have changed. By now, there are so many Israelites, the Egyptians are starting to feel more than a little crowded, and tensions run high between the two groups.

There get to be so many Israelites living in Egypt that the new Pharaoh feels threatened. He has no clue who Joseph was or what a big deal he was to the previous king. So he becomes ruthless, saying, "We can't let these foreigners keep prospering. It's us or them! Tell you what—let's make them our slaves!"

> So the Egyptians made the Israelites their slaves. They appointed brutal slave drivers over them, hoping to wear them down with crushing labor…So the Egyptians worked the people of Israel without mercy. They made their lives bitter…They were ruthless in all their demands (Exodus 1:11-14).

But the Hebrews in Egypt keep multiplying. Since his big "enslave our neighbors initiative" didn't work, Pharaoh decides on a more extreme solution—kill them. Not the adult slaves (the pyramids weren't going to build themselves, you know). No, they would just kill the babies. In fact, just the boy babies. Drown them in the Nile River the minute they are born. That's more cold-blooded than a crocodile.

God Remembers

In the face of this evil, the Israelite slaves cry out, "God, where are you? You promised Abraham you would look after his people and make us a great nation, but here we are, slaves in a foreign land, so far away from our promised home. Do you care? Do you even notice?"

God notices. He remembers. He cares. He sees their plight and listens to their prayers. He decides to rescue them by...sending a baby. (Interesting strategy. Let's see if it pays off.)

One day, a Hebrew couple gives birth to a little boy. They name him Moses and defy Pharaoh's law by keeping the boy alive. But they can't hide him at home because Egyptian soldiers are going house to house, looking for Hebrew baby boys to throw in the river. So Moses's parents take him to the last place anyone would look for a baby—the river.

They put Moses in a waterproof basket and hide him among the reeds on the bank of the Nile. They hope the trick will give them time to think of a way to get Moses to safety. Or maybe for God to do something awesome. Moses's older sister, Miriam, hides nearby to see what will happen.

And awesome is just the right word for what happens next.

A daughter of Pharaoh (yep, her dad was King "Kill 'Em All" himself) notices the basket in the river and discovers the baby inside. "Poor little fella!" she says. "He will die here in the river! Why don't I take him home with me and raise him in the palace?"

Seizing her chance, Miriam steps out of the reeds. "Ahem...Your Highness? If you're looking for help, I happen to know someone who is amazing with kids." And Miriam goes to get Moses's mother.

Do you see the hand of God at work? Against all odds, Moses is rescued, his mother gets to take care of him, and he is raised in the royal court of Pharaoh as a prince instead of a slave. This rescue operation is only a taste of things to come.

Moses Takes a Detour

Moses gets bored living in the palace all the time. He has a hankering to get out, see the real world, meet new people—especially his Hebrew relatives. So he ventures outside the palace walls. What he sees is horrifying. Injustice. Brutality. The misery of people in the bonds of slavery. It ends up being too much for Moses to handle.

When Moses sees an Egyptian slave driver beating an Israelite slave, Moses goes into a rage and kills the slave driver. Terrified, Moses buries him and makes a run for it back to the palace, hoping nobody saw what he did.

But it's too late. The secret is out. Everyone knows. Even the Pharaoh. Gulp.

Moses runs. (Wouldn't you?)

He runs clear to Midian (in modern Saudi Arabia). He isn't in a beautiful palace anymore. He is in an ugly desert. And to survive in a desert, you have to live like the desert people. So Moses, born a slave and raised a prince, becomes a shepherd. He also gets married and starts a family. And out in the desert day after day, for forty long years, he thinks.

While he is in the desert thinking, things in Egypt are changing.

> Years passed, and the king of Egypt died. But the Israelites continued to groan under their burden of slavery. They cried out for help, and their cry rose up to God. God heard their groaning, and he remembered his covenant promise to Abraham, Isaac, and Jacob. He looked down on the people of Israel and knew it was time to act (Exodus 2:23-25).

God has rescued Moses twice—once after he was born, and again after he killed the slave driver. Have you wondered why God keeps rescuing Moses?

GOD RESCUES MOSES TO RESCUE ISRAEL

The Burning Bush

It's time for God to tell Moses The Plan—God's plan to free the Israelites from Egypt so they can return to the Promised Land. The plan sounds like good news for Moses...at first.

> One day Moses...led the flock far into the wilderness and came to Sinai, the Mountain of God. There the angel of the LORD appeared to him in a blazing fire from the middle of a bush. Moses stared in amazement. Though the bush was engulfed in flames, it didn't burn up. "This is amazing," Moses said to himself. "Why isn't this bush burning up? I must go see it."
>
> When the LORD saw Moses coming to take a closer look, God called to him from the middle of the bush, "Moses! Moses!"

"Here I am!" Moses replied.

"Do not come any closer," the LORD warned. "Take off your sandals, for you are standing on holy ground. I am the God of your father—the God of Abraham, the God of Isaac, and the God of Jacob." When Moses heard this, he covered his face because he was afraid to look at God.

Then the LORD told him, "I have certainly seen the oppression of my people in Egypt. I have heard their cries of distress because of their harsh slave drivers. Yes, I am aware of their suffering. So I have come down to rescue them from the power of the Egyptians and lead them out of Egypt into their own fertile and spacious land" (Exodus 3:1-8).

Moses is thrilled. You can imagine him thinking, "Yes! All right! God hasn't forgotten us! He's finally going to rescue my people!"

That's the good news. Here's the bad news for Moses: "Now go, for I am sending you to Pharaoh" (Exodus 3:10).

Oh boy. This is not Moses's idea of a good time. He hasn't spent half a lifetime in the desert thinking, "Hey, it sure would be nice to go back to Egypt, see the Pharaoh, who totally wants to kill me, and tell him to let go of all his slaves. It'll be just like old times!"

So Moses makes excuses. "Why me?" he asks. "I'm a wanted man! I haven't seen Egypt for forty years. The people I'd be trying to save won't even remember me, and the people who do remember me want me dead!"

But God answers, "I will be with you."

Moses tries again. "If the Israelites ask me, 'Who sent you?' what am I supposed to say? 'God sent me'? They haven't had so much as a postcard from you in four hundred years! They may not even remember you!"

But God says, "You tell them, 'I Am.' I am the God of Abraham, the God of Isaac, the God of Jacob. I am the promise-making God, I am the promise-keeping God, I am the rescuing God. I do not change, no matter how long you wait for me. I. Am. Period."

Moses goes for excuse number three. "What if they *still* won't believe me?"

But God answers, "I've got you covered. I'll give you power to do miracles. That will get their attention."

Moses reaches the bottom of his bag of excuses and scrapes up one more: "I don't talk good! Me bad at word-saying. See?"

But God replies, "I will teach you what to say! Lesson one: It's 'I don't speak *well*.'"

Moses, out of excuses and dreading a divine grammar lesson, finally says what he really means.

"O Lord, I don't want to go to Egypt! Please, please, please, don't make me go. Send *anybody* but me!"

Though God's patience is infinite, Moses seems to be testing it.

So God says, "Okay, okay. I'll let you win this one. You don't have to speak. Your brother Aaron can do the talking for you. But you still have to go. And you will have to tell Aaron what to say."

Moses decides that facing death is easier than public speaking, so he does what God says. He leaves Midian with his family, meets his brother in the desert, and brings Aaron up to speed on the burning bush conversation. Then the two of them take their duo act to Egypt. Aaron speaks God's message. Moses performs miracles. And the people of Israel all worship the Lord.

The Exodus

In any good story with a hero like Moses, there's got to be a villain lurking in the shadows.

Enter Pharaoh, Ramses II, son of the sun god!

Unlike the Hebrews, who believed their God to be the one and only God, the ancient Egyptians had a bunch of gods, including the sun (the most powerful of all their gods) and Pharaoh himself, the sun's son. (It's confusing, we know.)

So God challenges Pharaoh to a contest to straighten things out. God says, "Pharaoh, I will send plagues on Egypt. Just try to stop them. Shouldn't be too hard, you being a god and everything."

Each plague challenges the powers Pharaoh claims to have over nature.

And now it's go time:

> Then the LORD said to Moses, "Get up early in the morning
> and stand before Pharaoh. Tell him, 'This is what the LORD,
> the God of the Hebrews, says: Let my people go, so they can
> worship me. If you don't, I will send more plagues on you and
> your officials and your people. Then you will know that there
> is no one like me in all the earth. By now I could have lifted
> my hand and struck you and your people with a plague to
> wipe you off the face of the earth. But I have spared you for
> a purpose—to show you my power and to spread my fame
> throughout the earth'" (Exodus 9:13-16).

God sends nine backbreaking plagues, but for a supposed sun-god's son,
Pharaoh is one coldhearted customer.

So God sends the tenth and final plague: A death angel comes for all the
firstborn sons in Egypt.

This plague is inescapable for anyone in the land, but the Israelites are
given a way out. Painting the door frames of their houses with the blood
of a lamb allows the angel of death to "pass over" the home. The Jewish
people remember that first Passover and celebrate it to this day.

This final plague, the death of his own son, breaks Pharaoh's hardened
heart. He finally gives up, telling Moses, "Enough! Your God wins! Get
out of my sight and take your pals with you, all several million of them."

The Israelites don't need to be told twice. They pack up and leave before Pharaoh can change his mind. Which Pharaoh does, almost immediately.

The refugees are camped out by the Red Sea, just outside of Egypt, when Pharaoh's army shows up to bring them back to slavery or death. There's nowhere to run. There's an army behind them, and they have no weapons. There's deep water ahead of them, and they have no boats. Things are grim. Understandably, the people freak out:

> As Pharaoh approached, the people of Israel looked up and panicked when they saw the Egyptians overtaking them. They cried out to the LORD, and they said to Moses, "Why did you bring us out here to die in the wilderness? Weren't there enough graves for us in Egypt?…Didn't we tell you this would happen while we were still in Egypt? We said, 'Leave us alone! Let us be slaves to the Egyptians. It's better to be a slave in Egypt than a corpse in the wilderness!'"

> But Moses told the people, "Don't be afraid. Just stand still and watch the LORD rescue you today. The Egyptians you see today will never be seen again. The LORD himself will fight for you. Just stay calm" (Exodus 14:10-14).

And here comes God to the rescue. He parts the waters of the sea and leads his people across on dry ground. The Egyptian army isn't so lucky. When they follow, the water comes rushing back in, drowning the pursuers.

God stays with his people as they cross the desert, placing a cloud in the sky by day and fire in the sky at night to guide them. He provides water from a rock when they are thirsty and gives manna from heaven when they are hungry.

God has rescued his children from slavery. But he's not finished.

GOD RESCUES ISRAEL TO RESCUE THE WORLD

God speaks to the whole nation of Israel from a volcano called Mount Sinai. There, he renews the promise he made to Abraham, and then he makes a new covenant with his people. In this covenant, God's part is to rescue Israel.

> The LORD called to [Moses] from the mountain and said, "Give these instructions to the family of Jacob; announce it to the descendants of Israel: 'You have seen what I did to the Egyptians. You know how I carried you on eagles' wings and brought you to myself'" (Exodus 19:3-4).

Israel also has a part to play in this covenant: to represent God in the world.

> Now if you will obey me and keep my covenant, you will be my own special treasure from among all the peoples on earth; for all the earth belongs to me. And you will be my kingdom of priests, my holy nation (Exodus 19:5-6).

All the nations in the world belong to God. Yet God chooses Israel for a special purpose—not to be an empire, but to be a kingdom of priests. A priest serves as a bridge between God and people.

Remember chapter 2? Listen again to the promise God made to Abram:

> I will make you into a great nation. I will bless you and make you famous, and you will be a blessing to others. I will bless those who bless you and curse those who treat you with contempt. All the families on earth will be blessed through you (Genesis 12:2-3).

God wants his chosen people to represent him to all people everywhere.

Which is where the Ten Commandments come in. They show the nation of Israel how to behave in the world in a way that sets them apart as God's representatives. The first four commands are about how they connect to God: "No other gods before me, no images of me, no name above my name, no day above my day."

The fifth command connects God with family: "Obey your parents, because they represent me."

The last five commands connect Israel to each other and to their neighbors in the world: "Don't take someone's life, don't take someone's husband or wife, don't take someone's possessions, don't fudge on the truth, and don't crave what others have."

By obeying these commands, the Israelites will look radically different from the people around them. And the nations will say, "We want to serve the God you serve!" Those who do not know God will be drawn to him by those who demonstrate his character.

Do you see the pattern here? God rescues Moses so Moses can rescue Israel and Israel can rescue the world. God does not rescue Moses for his sake or Israel for her sake. He rescues both for the world's sake.

That is still God's pattern.

SLAVE OR FREE?

By grace, God rescues you. Through the sacrificial death and triumphant resurrection of Jesus, you are made free. The question is, are you living as a free person?

In the beginning, God created nothing evil. Everything God made was good because God is good. But because sin is evil, every good thing can be twisted or distorted. What God intended for good, the evil one disfigured. Every heavenly gift now has a hellish shadow side.

These twisted gifts fight for your attention. They compete for your allegiance. They struggle for your very soul. And they aren't satisfied until you fall on your knees and worship them. When that happens, they have become your gods. They are your idols. They own you.

 ## WHO IS YOUR MASTER?

Anything that owns you is your master, and even good things will turn cruel when you give them ultimate power over your life. Popularity, money, power, having lots of stuff—none of those are good rulers when they become your idols. When they are lord of your life, they are not kind and loving. They are demonic and destructive.

Jesus came to rescue you from these false gods. And as we have seen with Abraham and Moses and Israel, God doesn't rescue you simply for your own sake. He rescues you so that you can rescue others—the kind of rescuing that comes from a heart of joy before God. The kind of rescuing that comes from a God-given desire to serve others.

 ## WHOM IS GOD CALLING YOU TO RESCUE?

Look around your home, your school, your neighborhood, and even the world. Whom are you being called to help?

God has not rescued you for your sake alone. You have been saved to serve. You have been rescued so you can be a rescuer. That is what chapter 3 in God's Great Story means to your story.

The Story Between the Story

One day while Moses is on Mount Sinai with God, the children of Israel go totally bonkers. In a classic act of people-pleasing, Aaron leads them in worshipping a golden calf, which ends badly for all involved. Moses gets angry, breaks two stone tablets that God had given him, sees the Lord's glory, gets a second set of tablets, and goes down the mountain with a bunch of laws so these sinful people will know how to live with a holy God.

Always faithful, God delivers his people right to the doorstep of an awesome new land, but they freak out over the big, nasty locals and say they'd rather go back to Egypt than trust the God who delivered them out of slavery in the first place. As punishment, the children of Israel wander in the wilderness for forty years until they all die off—except for Joshua and Caleb, who never doubted God's goodness.

After Moses dies, God chooses Joshua as the new leader of his people and gives him the green light to take the Promised Land. Reports of God's power and glory have the big, nasty locals quaking in their boots, and with the help of an unlikely ally named Rahab, the children of Israel finally cross the Jordan River, take the city of Jericho, and enter the Promised Land, just like God intended forty years earlier.

The next few hundred years are a cycle of backsliding, defeat, and God's gracious deliverance of his hardheaded, hard-hearted people. God provides judges to help deliver them, including Deborah, Gideon, and Samuel. Never satisfied, the children of Israel want to be like the cool kids and have a monarchy, so God relents and gives them King Saul, who proves they really should be careful what they wish for.

And that, in a nutshell, is the story between the story.

4

God Chooses

If you were going to draw a picture of a king, it would probably turn out looking a lot like Saul. He has it all—he is tall and strong and looks good in a gold crown. It is Israel's first try at having a king, and everyone thinks Saul will be the perfect guy to sit on the throne and make the big decisions. Unfortunately, Saul can't live up to the picture everyone has painted of him. He is impatient, angry, jealous, and convinced someone is out to get him. He is so bad at being king, God has to fire him and start over with a brand-new leader.

God sends Samuel, his right-hand man and talent scout, to the house of a man named Jesse in a little nowhere town called Bethlehem to kick off the first season of "Israel's Next Top Monarch."

Samuel is totally surprised when God doesn't send Eliab, the oldest of Jesse's eight sons, on to the final round. Just like Saul, he totally looks like a king! But the Lord hits the big red X button on him *and* the next six contestants (his younger brothers).

Samuel gets a little worried. He asks Jesse to send in son number eight, even though the kid has been out tending sheep and isn't ready for any kind of close-up. When scruffy little David makes it to the big stage, God tells Samuel to break out the golden buzzer: David is his choice to lead his people.

David, a small-time shepherd boy from a one-horse town, is put on the fast track to fame, fortune, and the most dramatic highs and lows imaginable. A highlight reel of David's life looks like this:

Thrilling victories! A one-shot kill against Goliath, the Philistine giant. Going full Indiana Jones and returning the ark of the covenant to Jerusalem. Leading the nation of Israel to the top of the Ancient World Leaderboard.

Terrible shame, scandal, and defeat! One bad decision after another takes David down a dark path of lies, adultery, and even murder.

And finally, tragedy! His own son Absalom rebels against him and tries to take over as the new king but ends up hanging from a tree by his own hair, looking like a pincushion. Even though Absalom had turned against him, David is devastated by the loss of his son.

David's time as king is pretty much over after Absalom dies. The last good thing he does after that is crown his son Solomon the next king... and that's David's chapter in God's Great Story!

Check out the official version of David's
story in 1 Samuel 16–31; 2 Samuel 1–23;
1 Kings 1–2; 1 Chronicles 11–28.

GOD'S STORY

God's Great Story is not a one-man show. Caring about others first is part of who God is, and he loves to share the stage, letting other characters reveal his purpose in their own personal way. Through David's own story, God reveals something surprising about himself. Can you guess what it is?

 ## GOD OFTEN CHOOSES THE LEAST EXPECTED

If you have ever been to vacation Bible school (VBS motto: Come for the snacks, stay for life-changing stories of God's purpose for your life!), you've heard about David, the shepherd boy who grows up to be someone God calls "a man after his own heart" (1 Samuel 13:14). It may seem like a no-brainer now, but at the time, it was a major surprise to everyone that God moved David to the front of the line. After all, David already had two big check marks by his name on the classroom whiteboard.

David Flunked the Birth-Order Test

In David's time, the firstborn son gets all the best jobs and privileges. He is always at the front of the line, he is in charge of all his brothers and sisters, and his allowance is twice as big as everyone else's. This isn't just something David's family does, it's basically the law! That's why Jesse doesn't even think to include David in the lineup to meet with Samuel in the first place. He is the youngest—the least in the eyes of the law.

And yet throughout God's Great Story, God ignores this law again and again. He passes over the firstborn and chooses the second son (or even the youngest) to take the lead role in some of his most important work.

That's why Samuel is stunned when God doesn't automatically pick Eliab as the new king that hot afternoon in Bethlehem. And when Samuel anoints David as the new king, it is a total surprise to everyone!

> For other stories of God turning the regular order upside down, look up Ishmael and Isaac, Esau and Jacob, and Reuben and Joseph in God's Great Story. In the New Testament, Jesus shakes up the normal way of doing things in his parable of the prodigal son, and also when he teaches his followers that "the last will be first, and the first will be last" (Matthew 20:16 NIV).

David Has Character Issues

You may have heard stories about David that make him seem like a perfect person. But over the course of his life, David was...complicated. (That's a nice way of saying that sometimes David does very, very bad things.) He commits adultery with another man's wife and then has her husband killed to cover up his sin. When it comes to those who oppose him, he can be ruthless, vindictive, and violent.

In spite of David's massive flaws, God uses him to do incredible things. David unifies the twelve tribes of Israel, makes the whole country richer than ever before, and brings back to life his people's worship of God. David's reign is a glorious point in Israel's history. Through the prophet Nathan, God tells David that one day a king from his line will establish a kingdom that never ends (2 Samuel 7:12-16). A thousand years later, when another baby is born in Bethlehem, the prophecy comes true. (You'll read about it in chapter 6.)

Don't miss this. God orchestrates all these things through a small-town sheep rancher's last-born son whose character failings would rival Saul's.

Surprising? Yes. But David isn't the first (or the last) suspicious character that God uses in a mighty way in his Great Story!

GOD'S STANDARD OF JUDGMENT

Now that we know David is...complicated, you might have some important questions. The biggest one is probably this: How can God use someone like David, who does some really bad things, to fulfill God's purpose?

The answer to that question has two parts. First, God does the best he can with who he's got. If he waited around for perfect people and worked only through them, he would be waiting forever. Second, God sees something in David that sets him apart from men like Saul, even when he messes up. That something is David's heart.

When Samuel is in Bethlehem with Jesse's sons lined up in front of him, God reminds him that God doesn't look at outside appearances, but at the truth of what is inside them. God says to Samuel, "Don't judge by his appearance or height, for I have rejected him. The LORD doesn't see things the way you see them. People judge by outward appearance, but the LORD looks at the heart" (1 Samuel 16:7).

What is it about David's heart that pleases God? A closer look at David's story reveals three things that convince God that David is the man for this moment in his Great Story.

God Chooses People Who Trust Him

When Israel was facing the Philistine army and trembling at the sight of their all-star warrior, Goliath, no one was willing to step up and take the challenge except David—not even big, tall King Saul. Saul didn't believe this small, idealistic teenager had a chance against the giant opponent, but David convinced him with this impassioned plea:

> I have been taking care of my father's sheep and goats...When a lion or bear comes to steal a lamb from the flock, I go after it with a club and rescue the lamb from its mouth. If the animal

> turns on me, I catch it by the jaw and club it to death. I have done this to both lions and bears, and I'll do it to this pagan Philistine, too, for he has defied the armies of the living God! The LORD who rescued me from the claws of the lion and the bear will rescue me from this Philistine (1 Samuel 17:34-37).

Remember the difference between faith and trust? Like Abraham, David doesn't just believe that God *can* fulfill his promises, he trusts that he *will*. God earned David's trust by helping him put together an undefeated record against the local bears and lions. Once you've taken down predators like those, taking on a lumbering giant in an open field is no big deal.

When David goes out to face Goliath, the big guy starts talking an even bigger game. He roars, "Am I a dog, that you come at me with a stick?" Goliath can't believe that Israel has sent out a pip-squeak little kid to fight him.

But David yells back, "You come at me with your puny weapons, but I've got the Lord of Heaven's Armies on my side. I'm going to kill you and cut off your head, and then my bros here are going to feed your friends to the birds. When we're done with you, the whole world will know that there is a God in Israel! Bring it!"

Lesson number one to Goliath: Never try to out trash-talk a teenager.

You know how the story ends. One well-aimed rock from David's sling hits Goliath right between the eyes, and the rest is history (1 Samuel 17:43-51).

David trusts God because God has proved himself faithful to David. As the book of Hebrews will one day say, "It is impossible to please God without faith" (Hebrews 11:6). No wonder God is drawn to David—he has buckets full of faith.

God Chooses People Who Have a Soft Heart

When you have the power to do whatever you want, whenever you want, and when you can destroy anyone who tries to stop you, it can be really easy to forget about God. David falls into the same traps that powerful people before him did and others still do today, but there is one major difference: More often than not, David's heart remains soft toward God.

At one of his lowest points, David takes advantage of Bathsheba, the wife of Uriah, one of his generals, and she becomes pregnant. It gets worse. Trying to hide what he has done, David fixes it so Uriah gets killed in battle. It seems David has forgotten how trying to hide from God worked out for Adam and Eve. It never goes well.

Before long the prophet Nathan comes knocking on David's door and tells him a quick story. It goes like this: Two men live in a certain town. One is rich and owns lots of sheep and cattle. The other is poor and owns nothing but a little lamb. That little lamb is precious to the man. It eats from his own plate and drinks from his own cup. The man loves the lamb like it is his own child. One day a guest comes to the home of the rich man. Instead of using a lamb from his own flock, he takes the poor man's lamb, kills it, and feeds it to his guest.

Does that story make you angry? It's unfair. It's horrible. It's mean and cruel. The rich man has absolutely no reason to do what he does, right?

David certainly thinks so. He's enraged! "Anyone who would do something like that deserves to die!" he says. Nathan lets David's statement hang in the air before laying down the hammer: "David, you are that man!" And David knows it now: He is the rich man. Uriah is the poor man. And he has not only stolen his wife, he has stolen his life.

What comes next is astounding. David makes no excuses. He doesn't blame Bathsheba for his actions. He doesn't accuse Nathan of spreading lies. He doesn't say, "If the king does it, it's not a bad thing." No, he owns it. He confesses, "I have sinned against the Lord."

> The whole David, Bathsheba, Uriah, and Nathan
> story can be found in 2 Samuel 11–12:14.

The depth of David's sorrow for this sin is on full display. It is expressed in the Bible like this:

> Have mercy on me, O God,
>   because of your unfailing love.
> Because of your great compassion,
>   blot out the stain of my sins.
> Wash me clean from my guilt.
>   Purify me from my sin.

> For I recognize my rebellion;
>> it haunts me day and night.
> Against you, and you alone, have I sinned;
>> I have done what is evil in your sight.
> You will be proved right in what you say,
>> and your judgment against me is just...
> Purify me from my sins, and I will be clean;
>> wash me, and I will be whiter than snow...
> Create in me a clean heart, O God.
>> Renew a loyal spirit within me.
> Do not banish me from your presence,
>> and don't take your Holy Spirit from me.
> Restore to me the joy of your salvation
>> and make me willing to obey you.
> Then I will teach your ways to rebels,
>> and they will return to you...
> You do not desire a sacrifice, or I would offer one.
>> You do not want a burnt offering.
> The sacrifice you desire is a broken spirit.
>> You will not reject a broken and repentant heart, O God
>> (Psalm 51:1-4,7,10-13,16-17).

What kind of person with unlimited power, who answers to no one, responds this way? What kind of person writes such a poignant confession? Only someone who has kept their heart soft toward God.

That's the secret to David's enduring relationship with God. He is a really big sinner, but he has a really soft heart.

God Chooses People Who Have a Deep Inner Life

As a shepherd, David's life is simple, but also super boring. Think about it—no Internet, no smartphones, no iPads, no video games, not even a library. There are only craggy hills, green pastures, starry skies, and an occasional wild animal or two. Oh, yeah…and God.

David takes advantage of his time alone in nature and devotes his attention to getting to know God. Just like at the dawn of creation, all creativity—speaking, listening, writing, reflecting, singing, and danc-ing—comes out of silence. It all flows out when you get to know the One who made it all. After sitting still with God, words like these can spring out of the heart and soul:

> O LORD, you have examined my heart
> > and know everything about me.
> You know when I sit down or stand up.
> > You know my thoughts even when I'm far away.
> You see me when I travel
> > and when I rest at home.
> > You know everything I do.
> You know what I am going to say
> > even before I say it, LORD.
> You go before me and follow me.
> > You place your hand of blessing on my head.
> Such knowledge is too wonderful for me,
> > too great for me to understand! (Psalm 139:1-6)

God gets to know David too. That's what David is celebrating in the lines from Psalm 139 above. In David's day, other nations worshipped gods that didn't care about humans. For a god to care about a person was unheard of. In the quiet wilderness, though, David comes to realize that God wants to know him too—his strengths and weaknesses, gifts and flaws, selflessness and selfishness. God knows David so completely that David can never hide anything from him, not even the very worst parts of himself. And God loves him, blesses him, and invites him into his grand adventure all the same.

Here's some really good news: God knows your life. All of it. Start to finish. Good and bad. And yes, he is inviting you into his epic story too. That may come as a huge surprise. You may feel like you were born in the wrong place, at the wrong time, or just wrong, period. All the ways you've ever messed up may be flashing in your brain as you're reading this. But God has a surprise for you: It doesn't matter how wrong you feel or how much you've messed up! If God can choose to use a man like David, he can use you to write a brand-new chapter in his ongoing story of redemption.

Remember, though, that while David had a long list of major sins, the three qualities we talked about (David's trust in God, his soft heart toward God, and his deep inner life) are essential for God to continue working in and through David.

ARE YOU TRUSTING GOD LIKE DAVID DID?

Trust is the foundation of our relationship with God.

As long as David trusts that God is with him and for him, his heart and soul remain open to God's presence, blessing, and correction. His life is like clay in the hands of a master sculptor. God can use him for his strategic purposes in the lives of his people.

The same can be true for us. The place to start is believing that God is for us and with us. When we trust, follow, and obey him, God knows that he can trust us too. And when God trusts you, he provides more opportunities to do his work.

IS YOUR HEART SOFT TOWARD GOD?

Wanting to do good doesn't mean we don't sometimes mess up. The apostle Paul once confessed, "I want to do what is right, but I can't. I want to do what is good, but I don't. I don't want to do what is wrong, but I do it anyway...Oh, what a miserable person I am!" (Romans 7:18-19,24).

God prefers that we make wise decisions 24/7. Since we don't, though, what matters next is how we respond when we mess up. Will we harden our hearts and insist we haven't done anything wrong? Will we place blame on someone else? Will we say that Mom and Dad haven't raised us well enough? Or instead, like David, will we turn to God with a soft heart, confess our failures, and ask for forgiveness? With a soft heart, we're playing on God's big stage again. With a hard heart, we're stuck on the sidelines.

ARE YOU CULTIVATING A DEEP INNER LIFE WITH GOD?

This can be the toughest challenge you face. Most people don't live out in nature anymore, where we can sit in quiet stillness. We have electronic devices, social media, and streaming content to binge-watch, all right at our fingertips. There's hardly any room left for God. So what do we do?

Like David, you must seek to live every moment of every day with a confidence that God is always by your side. Whisper words to him. Listen for his voice. Keep David's words, the Psalms, running through your mind and heart. Draw strength from God and slay the giants standing between you and the life he intends for you.

If you can do these things, you, too, will be a person after God's own heart.

The Story Between the Story

David is a great king and a man after God's own heart, but his family is *crazy* dysfunctional. After David's death, God chooses his son Solomon to lead the nation and blesses Solomon with great wisdom. It's an age of peace and prosperity for Israel. But despite his wisdom, Solomon buys into the lie that more is better, and he starts worshipping many false gods.

After Solomon's death it's pretty much all downhill for Israel. Civil war divides the nation. The northern kingdom keeps the name Israel, the southern kingdom takes the name Judah, and a procession of weak and idolatrous kings encourages God's people to worship false gods. This is a decision that ends badly for just about everyone.

There are a few bright spots, however. A boy-king named Josiah leads an extreme makeover of the Temple. King Jehoshaphat routs an enemy army—not by fighting but by singing. King Hezekiah trusts God, who defeats another enemy army with no help whatsoever.

Yet the bad kings always outnumber the good kings, leading the people astray. That's why, through the years, God sends prophets like Elijah, Elisha, and Isaiah to remind the people of God's faithful love and to warn them of the consequences of their sin. But the people love their false gods way too much to listen to the one true God. Time after time, despite the warnings of the prophets, the beloved children of Israel mercilessly break God's heart. Because of their stubborn disobedience, God finally allows his people to experience his judgment.

And that, in a nutshell, is the story between the story.

5

God Warns

You may have noticed a pattern by now, a major thread that weaves through God's Great Story. It's a pattern of highs and lows. God makes a big promise to be there for his people, and the people follow God for a while and experience incredible blessings. But then people start to forget about God's promise, and they suffer incredible loss. Eventually someone comes along to remind God's people of his promise to them and leads them back to the way God laid out for them.

After the reigns of David and Solomon, this pattern of highs and lows reaches its lowest point since the days of Egypt. Within a few hundred years of David's incredible time as king, the nation of Israel is almost completely destroyed, and its people are scattered into exile thousands of miles away from the land God promised his people, in a place called Babylon (pronounced "Babble On" in case you were wondering).

But even when things are at their lowest (and boy, do things get pretty low!), God is not standing by, doing nothing. He sends his prophets (God's professional truth-tellers) to remind his people of the promises he made with Abraham and with Moses. Here's the short version: "If you obey, you will prosper. If you disobey, you will perish."

> The longer version is in Deuteronomy 28. The first 14 verses tell about the ways God will bless his people if they obey. The rest of the chapter describes the dire consequences they can expect if they disobey and turn away from him. It's not a pretty picture.

Just like when a parent counts to three to give a misbehaving child a chance to stop throwing a tantrum, God gives the Israelites chance after chance to make better choices. He doesn't just count to three, he counts to 208...years. That's how long, after Solomon died, God gives Israel to get its act together. Israel's sister nation, Judah, gets another 136 years after that. (You'd think Judah would have taken the hint after Israel gets its supreme spanking, but no.) And while God is counting, he sends prophets to give his people plenty of warning to get back on track. These prophets, as you will soon see, are a colorful collection of characters to say the least.

GOD'S STORY

People like to focus on how prophets are able to predict the future, which is a cool ability, we admit. But while prophets do sometimes talk about distant future events, like the coming of the Messiah, they spend literally 98 percent of their time talking about things that impact people in the present.

With that in mind, let's explore how God uses the prophets in his Great Story.

THE PURPOSE OF THE PROPHETS— GOD'S EARLY WARNING SYSTEM

Whenever a big storm comes our way, weather people (or meteorologists, if you're fancy) with special radar equipment track its path and use the information they gather to predict where the storm will go, how big it will get, and whether people need to stay put or run for cover. Prophets do basically the same thing, but instead of weather patterns, they pay attention to the condition and direction of people's hearts, their communities, and their nation as a whole. They could predict when danger is on its way and then tell people what they needed to do to survive and even thrive through their covenant relationship with God.

MAJORS AND MINORS: THE PROPHET LINEUP

There is a whole lineup of prophets in the Bible. Some of them—fifteen to be exact—wrote parts of the Old Testament, beginning with Isaiah and ending with Malachi. The Bible divides these writers into (three) major and (twelve) minor prophets. This doesn't mean the major prophets were way better at their job—just that they wrote longer books than the minors.

Other prophets may not have written any books at all; instead, they did things that other people wrote about. You heard about some of them already, like Moses, who freed the children of Israel from Egyptian slavery; Samuel, who led the people before Israel had kings; and Nathan, who guided David. Then there's Elijah, who had the BBQ to end all BBQs on the top of Mount Carmel. Four or five women are also named as prophets—Miriam, Deborah, Huldah, the wife of Isaiah (who might have been Huldah), and Noadiah.

Here's a quick look at a few of the major and minor prophets. Isaiah (who lived around 740 BC) may have been part of the royal family and lived in Jerusalem among the elite members of his society. Either he really got into his work or he needed constant reminders of what to tell people, because he named his kids after his most important prophecies. There was Shear-jashub, which means "a remnant shall return"; Immanuel, which means "God with us"; and finally, Maher-Shalal-Hash-Baz, the longest name in the Old Testament, which means "spoil quickly, plunder speedily"—a heads-up about the coming invasion of the Assyrians. (Or maybe Maher-Shalal-Hash-Baz was just always leaving the refrigerator door open; it's hard to say.)

Jeremiah (circa 626 BC) was probably not invited to a lot of parties; he could be a real downer to hang out with. Jeremiah was mad at everyone and everything around him—even at God at one point for making him a prophet in the first place. (He really wanted to be a dancer! Okay, not really. But he sure didn't like his regular job.) He smashed pots. He cried a lot. He got fed up with God's people breaking their covenant agreement. So finally, he told them that one day God would cancel the whole deal and make a new one. (More on that later.)

Then there was Ezekiel, who lived around the same time as Jeremiah. His approach to being a prophet was a little more...artistic. Every day, Ezekiel would stand in front of the Temple of Jerusalem and pretend to destroy it. It was a huge hit. His one-man show, "Our Temple Is Going to Be Destroyed One Day," ran for years, right up until the Babylonians showed up and destroyed the Temple.

God uses these three prophets, along with the other twelve, to warn his people of the judgment coming their way if they do not turn their hearts back to him. To understand the story God tells through the prophets, it's important to know what the prophets are really trying to say when they delivered messages to his people.

GOD COMMUNICATES A CONSISTENT MESSAGE

The Prophets Call Out Sinful Behavior

The people of Israel and Judah forget about their promise to God over time and start to think they don't need God's blessing at all. They turn to other gods and idols, hoping to get an even better deal than what God was offering. You can imagine how that turns out. God's prophets try to warn the people about what will happen if they continue to turn away from God and worship false idols—and all of the prophets agree that it wouldn't be pretty.

Even though God takes sin seriously, his heart is full of love for his people. It hurts God when he sees them making choices that cause harm to themselves and others. You might even say it breaks his heart.

> Therefore, go and give this message to Israel. This is what the Lord says:
>
> "O Israel, my faithless people,
>   come home to me again,
> for I am merciful.
>   I will not be angry with you forever.
> Only acknowledge your guilt...
> And I will give you shepherds after my own heart,
>   who will guide you with knowledge and understanding"
>   (Jeremiah 3:12-13,15).

The Prophets Warn of Future Consequences

After calling out Israel's or Judah's guilt, the prophets foretell the consequences awaiting those who had turned their backs on God and his covenant. They tell God's people about the future to try to change their thoughts and behaviors in the present. Those who refuse to repent and turn back to God will get smacked with judgment. Those who do repent get a promise of salvation and blessing:

This is what the LORD of Heaven's Armies, the God of Israel, says:

> "Even now, if you quit your evil ways, I will let you stay in your own land. But don't be fooled by those who promise you safety simply because the LORD's Temple is here…I will be merciful only if you stop your evil thoughts and deeds and start treating each other with justice; only if you stop exploiting foreigners, orphans, and widows; only if you stop your murdering; and only if you stop harming yourselves by worshiping idols. Then I will let you stay in this land that I gave to your ancestors to keep forever" (Jeremiah 7:3-7).

Pay close attention to what is happening here. These predictions are not what God wants to happen. Not at all! The predictions are a warning against danger. When your parents taught you to look both ways before crossing the street, they may have told you that if you don't follow that rule, you could get hit by a car. That's a scary warning when you think about it! But it's there to keep you safe and healthy. God's warnings work the same way.

The Prophets Promise Hope

Even though God's people chase after other gods again and again, his love never goes away. He can't wait for the day that they return to him and are restored in his goodness. Each prophet, in his own place and time, offers a beautiful vision of what redemption and restoration will look like. Here is a hope-giving example from the prophet Jeremiah:

> "In that day," says the LORD, "I will be the God of all the families of Israel, and they will be my people..."

Long ago the LORD said to Israel:

> "I have loved you, my people, with an everlasting love.
>   With unfailing love I have drawn you to myself"
>   (Jeremiah 31:1-3).

Even after all the chances God has given them, after hundreds of years of warnings through the prophets, Israel doesn't listen. The people's hearts do not change. Because God's love is based on allowing people to choose whether to obey, the time finally comes to let the consequences of their actions arrive.

Speaking through Isaiah, God expresses his frustration with his people. He has done everything he could for them. He has given them a home, a place to grow into the nation that would one day bless the whole world. "What more could I have done for my vineyard that I have not already done?" (Isaiah 5:4).

> Read the short parable of the
> vineyard in Isaiah 5:1-7.

God answers his own question by promising to do two brand-new things. First, he is going to send a Messiah, an anointed one who will save his people and create a new kingdom of people, a new Israel from out of the old one. Isaiah delivers the good news of God's plan:

> For a child is born to us,
>> a son is given to us.
> The government will rest on his shoulders.
>> And he will be called:
> Wonderful Counselor, Mighty God,
>> Everlasting Father, Prince of Peace
>> (Isaiah 9:6).

The second new thing God is going to do is have the Messiah make a new covenant with his people. The covenant with Moses had a problem. God's faithfulness was never in doubt, but the grip of sin on God's people was so tight that they could never live up to their part of the agreement. So once again, God steps in to help.

In the New Testament, the book of Hebrews quotes the prophet Jeremiah's announcement of a new covenant. It then explains the *why* behind God's actions (there's that *why* question again!):

> If the first covenant had been faultless, there would have been no need for a second covenant to replace it…
>
> > "But this is the new covenant I will make
> >> with the people of Israel on that day, says the LORD:
> > I will put my laws in their minds,
> >> and I will write them on their hearts.
> > I will be their God, and they will be my people…

And I will forgive their wickedness,
and I will never again remember their sins."

When God speaks of a "new" covenant, it means he has made
the first one obsolete. It is now out of date and will soon dis-
appear (Hebrews 8:7-13).

The covenant God made with Israel through Moses was indeed gracious.
The Lord came through on his promise and rescued his people from slavery in Egypt. But after that, Israel received the benefits of the covenant
only if they were faithful. If they disobeyed, they paid. In the story so far,
we see how often God's people were unable to live up to their promises.

As good as the covenant with Moses was, it was not able to transform
the hearts of God's people. So it had to go.

God's new covenant is different. It is between God and all people on
the earth, not just Israel. Jesus, the Messiah, will do what we as human
beings can't. He will keep the agreement so perfectly that his actions
will count for all of us. Because of Jesus, this new covenant is uncon-
ditional! God's grace and blessings flow down from heaven to all of us!
That is incredibly good news, and it makes up the next chapter in God's
Great Story—and what a chapter it is!

But first...

Remember the pattern we talked about at the start of the chapter? The thread of highs and lows, ups and downs, that weaves through God's Great Story? That thread runs through our story today. We are living 2,700 years after the prophets wrote, but our stories aren't much different from the ones spoken by the oracles of long ago. Only the names and places have changed.

WORSHIPPING IDOLS

Everywhere you look, advertisements are trying to sell you the next big thing. They make you feel like something is missing in your life (which may be true) and that their product will fix everything (which is almost certainly not true). But the advertisements can be very convincing! It's fun to have the best new toy, or the latest video game, or the coolest clothes.

But the excitement and fun of those things always wears off. And we're right back in the same spot we were in before we had those things. So we look for the next new, shiny thing to make us feel good. Over and over again. We start to think that the solution to all our problems comes from having a lot of *things*. But that's a lie. When we fall for it, just like the Israelites of old, we make an idol of *things* and turn our backs on the only One who can fulfill us.

SUFFERING THE CONSEQUENCES

Unlike God, material things are temporary. They can break, wear out, or go away without warning. Putting our ultimate trust in temporary things never ends well.

So God's love can be tough. He allows us to experience the full consequences of our mistakes when we live as if he doesn't exist—disappointment, despair, brokenness, shame, guilt, regret, emptiness, loneliness, and finally, death.

But there's hope! Just as in the day of the prophets, God's tough love is meant to save us, not punish us. God lets us mess up so we can learn from our mistakes and turn to him.

THE WAY BACK

God cares for his people. He sent the prophets to warn them of the consequences of their unfaithfulness, hoping they would return to him. When they refused to listen, God did not enjoy the consequences of their disobedience. His heart was broken. When the consequences came to Israel, God suffered right along with his people.

You will see in the next chapter how God's goodness is going to lead people back to himself.

Before you move on to the next chapter, though, take a little bit of time to do some thinking.

Are there any things in your life that you are treating like an idol? How do you feel when those things break or let you down? What is it about those things that have power over you?

Now, think about what it would feel like if you were released from the power those things hold over you. Imagine being truly free. Dream about being saved from your very worst self and discovering the secret to becoming your very best self...and you'll be ready to learn how God saves.

The Story Between the Story

As it turns out, God's chosen people are disobedient little stinkers who have pretty much hit rock bottom. Their Promised Land is seized by foreign powers, Solomon's beautiful temple is destroyed, and God's people are led away into exile. Among the Jews living in exile decades later are two great men named Ezra and Nehemiah. Ezra (a priest) leads a group of Israelites in Babylon to return to Jerusalem, rebuild the temple, and turn back to God. Nehemiah joins them from Persia and inspires the people to rebuild the city wall in just fifty-two days. Thanks to God's faithfulness through Ezra and Nehemiah, the children of Israel still remaining in exile now have a home to return to. But God still has something even better up his sleeve.

Many of the Jewish people return to their homeland, but the nation will never again return to the political prominence it enjoyed under its great kings. For centuries, God's people endure oppression under foreign rule by the Persians, then the Greeks, and then the Romans. The Temple is desecrated, and the prophets grow silent.

But despite the silence, deep in the hearts of the children of Israel, hope whispers. The people remember the prophecies of Isaiah and Jeremiah. They remember God's promises of deliverance through his Chosen One—a Messiah who would break the yoke of slavery. As centuries pass, God's people begin to imagine their Messiah will be another David—a great military leader who will break the oppression of their foreign overlords. But what they seem to miss is that the prophecies also subtly point to a different kind of Savior—one who would be despised and rejected. A man of sorrows who is acquainted with deepest grief and led like a lamb to slaughter. What kind of Messiah is this?

After centuries of silence from God and oppression from foreign powers, God's people are desperately watching for something big to happen. And finally, it does. But it comes in such an altogether unexpected way that many of them miss it completely.

And that, in a nutshell, is the story between the story.

Jesus

UNDER FOREIGN RULE

Persians

Greeks

Romans

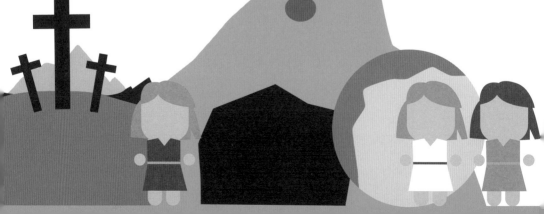

6

God Saves

God has come to save us! Hurray!

But before God saves us, he becomes one of us. That miracle happens when a certain baby boy is born in Bethlehem. An angel tells his parents what to name him: "Give him the name Jesus, because he will save his people from their sins" (Matthew 1:21 NIV).

Herod the Great (but really the Not So Great) goes all Pharaoh from the Old Testament and tries to kill the baby Jesus before he can grow up to be a king. But God foils Herod, and Jesus is whisked away to safety in the land of Egypt (what a twist!).

Jesus and his family return to Israel when that Herod dies and his sons (also named Herod) split up his territory. Jesus grows up in a tight-knit Jewish family in Nazareth, a small village in Galilee.

Around age thirty, Jesus makes his first big public appearance. He gets baptized in the Jordan River by his cousin John (a.k.a. John the Baptizer) and then heads straight to the desert to connect with God. After forty days with nothing to eat, a tired and hungry Jesus is confronted by Satan, who offers him power and fame if Jesus will turn his back on God's plan. Jesus is able to resist the temptation and sends the devil packing. (Why didn't the devil start by offering him a sandwich? We don't know. Let's just say Lucifer isn't the brightest star in the morning sky.)

In the lake town of Capernaum, Jesus calls twelve locals to be his disciples. Over the next three years, crowds show up to celebrate Jesus, gawk at his miracles, and praise his message—but they don't all step up and put his teachings into action. They like being around him, but his example of serving others and embracing pain is too hard for them to practice.

In early 30 AD, Jesus leaves Galilee for the big city of Jerusalem. He tells the disciples they're going there for Passover, but he knows something even bigger is going to happen. When they arrive in Jerusalem, mobs of people crowd the streets. It's the Passover celebration—a huge block party and political protest all at the same time.

Jesus rides into town on a donkey. It's wild. The crowds go nuts over him. They scream and shout for him to save them from the Romans, who are running their country and making their lives miserable.

The religious rulers feel threatened by Jesus. The crowds want to crown Jesus as their king. But that would make Caesar—the emperor of Rome, ruler of the known world, and not a great sharer—very, very mad at them.

Like "burn the city to the ground and not leave one stone standing on top of another" mad.

The religious rulers don't want that to happen. (Jerusalem has been wasted before. Remember chapter 5?) The local Roman authorities don't want that to happen either. (There's so much paperwork when a city is burned to the ground.) So the religious leaders of Jerusalem and the political leaders of Rome get together and come up with a plan to kill the only truly good man who has ever lived.

And they do. On a hill outside the city gates, on a Friday afternoon, Jesus gives up his life.

But on the third day, God surprises everyone. He raises Jesus back to life. Jesus convinces his twelve disciples that he isn't a ghost and tells them to spread the word. Fifty days later, Jesus returns to heaven to be with his Father. Mission accomplished.

> **Check out these famous verses from the four Gospels that affirm that God saves:**
>
> Matthew 1:21   Luke 2:11; 10:19
> Mark 10:45   John 3:16-17; 12:47

Before Jesus arrives, the people of Israel go hundreds of years without hearing from God. Is God ignoring them? Is he neglecting them? Did he forget them?

God does not forget his promise—he just waits for the right time to make his move. And when that time comes, boy oh boy, does he move.

"But when the right time came, God sent his Son" (Galatians 4:4).

God's plan is laid out to the last detail. He sends Jesus to a particular place, at a particular time, to a particular people. We need to understand the time, place, and people if we want to understand Jesus.

That's why we turn to the Jewish story first—so we can understand the Jesus story.

 ## THE JEWISH STORY

Israel has always been a tiny nation. If it were part of the United States, it would be one of the smallest states—about the size of New Jersey or Vermont.

God's covenant people were originally called "Israelites." They were nicknamed "Jews" (from the word "Judea") when they were exiled to Babylon in 586 BC. The name stuck. Jews who live in modern Israel call themselves Israelis.

Israel's neighbors were much bigger. Major superpowers, like Egypt, Syria, Babylon (Iraq), and Persia (Iran), kicked Israel around like a soccer ball.

When Jesus goes into Galilee "proclaiming the good news of God" (Mark 1:14 NIV), his fellow Jews haven't heard any good news for a long time. They have been ruled by the Persians, the Greeks, and now the Romans, whose soldiers abuse the Jewish people just because they can.

Being bullied nonstop for hundreds of years made the Israelites feel terribly alone in the world. They hoped for their oppression to end, praying that God would send them a deliverer—the Messiah, who would save them all. They seek to be faithful to God the best they can. Under Roman oppression, this faithfulness takes different forms.

Politics in Jesus's Day

Politics and religion were not separated in first-century Palestine like they are in America today. Religious groups acted like political parties. Like today, those parties had a hard time agreeing on anything. Here's a quick look at those groups.

- *The Sadducees.* (Motto: Let's compromise!) They will do anything to keep Rome happy and Israel safe, even if it means
  going against their religious beliefs. They're in charge of the
  Sanhedrin (kind of the Jewish Supreme Court).

- *The Pharisees.* (Motto: Never compromise!) Totally oppo-
  site from the Sadducees. They follow the law of Moses to a
  T. They consider non-Jewish people (a.k.a. Gentiles, a.k.a.
  Romans) to be dirtier than pigs in mud. They will not compromise their faith. Period.

- *The Zealots.* (Motto: What is compromise?) These guys are
  always ready for a fight. They hate Romans, period, and will
  do anything to get them out of Israel. They believe that freedom is worth any price—even if innocent people have to pay
  for it.

- *The Essenes.* (Motto: Let's make like the Red Sea and part
  ways!) They decide living under Roman rule gets in the way
  of their favorite thing—reading the law of Moses. So they
  head out to the desert beyond the Dead Sea, where they
  start communes devoted to studying, praying, and living
  disciplined lives. They were not the most popular group.

- *Average Jews.* (Motto: We're busy being oppressed. Call us
  when you figure it out.) Like most people, they're just trying to live. Ninety percent of Jews in Jesus's day are farm-
  ers, shepherds, day laborers, and merchants. They feed their

families, obey God to the best of their ability, and try to stay out of the Romans' way.

Whatever their differences, these groups all have one thing in common: They want their freedom. They want God to fulfill his promise to Abraham. They want God to send a new Moses to rescue them. They want God to raise up a new David who will defeat their enemies. They want God to send them a Messiah, a Deliverer, a King.

This is the world Jesus enters.

 ## THE JESUS STORY

Anonymity

Jesus's birth almost goes unnoticed, which is weird for a king.

An unknown teenager named Mary learns from an angel that she's going to get pregnant through the power of God's Spirit. After an awkward conversation with her soon-to-be-husband, Joseph, and a long walk to backwater Bethlehem, Mary gives birth to Jesus in a smelly barn with no one around but some confused critters who aren't used to sharing their food trough with a sleeping baby. Not exactly a royal welcome.

No one else will know who Jesus is for another thirty years.

Popularity

Jesus's public ministry begins when his cousin John baptizes him in the Jordan River. John resists at first because his baptism is for people who want to change their ways from evil to good, and he knows Jesus doesn't need that. Jesus persuades him to do it anyway. When Jesus comes up out of the water, a voice from heaven calls out, "You are my Son, whom I love; with you I am well pleased" (Mark 1:11 NIV). And the power of God's Spirit surrounds him.

Jesus then goes into the nearby Judean desert. He prays for strength to follow God's path for him because it will be hard and painful. The evil one appears, trying to talk him into taking an easier way—the road of popularity, fame, and power. Jesus resists.

Then things really get started.

> Jesus went into Galilee, where he preached God's Good News.
> "The time promised by God has come at last!" he announced.
> "The Kingdom of God is near" (Mark 1:14-15).

What that means is, "You won't believe what God has in store for you. It's what you've been waiting for your whole life. It's so close you can touch it. In fact, he's looking at you right now."

Jesus does more than offer God's Kingdom to everyone. He also invites people to follow him as he is following God.

> One day as Jesus was walking along the shore of the Sea of Galilee, he saw two brothers—Simon, also called Peter, and Andrew—throwing a net into the water, for they fished for a living. Jesus called out to them, "Come, follow me" (Matthew 4:18-19).

Many accept his invitation. They follow him. They learn from him. They become his disciples. People finally take notice of Jesus of Nazareth.

For the next two years, his popularity soars. Almost everyone loves him. Why? What makes people want to be with him?

Jesus's Miracles

It doesn't hurt that Jesus performs miracles. Almost forty are listed in the first four books of the New Testament, which tell Jesus's story. Each miracle shows God's power. Each one meets a human need. Each one gives a glimpse of heaven on earth. But they come in different flavors.

Some miracles show Jesus's power over nature, like the time he is in a small boat with his disciples on the Sea of Galilee. It's late at night, a furious storm erupts, and everyone is scared to death. Everyone except Jesus. He silences the storm and calms the waves (Matthew 8:23-27). Child's play.

Some miracles show his power over sickness. He heals a man with leprosy. Lepers in Jesus's day are outcasts that no one will even touch. Yet Jesus touches the man, demonstrating God's compassion for humans. It is also a preview for the future, when sickness, disease, and death will be distant memories (Matthew 8:1-4).

Some miracles show that he is stronger than evil. One time he casts a legion of demons out of a man who is strong as an ox, crazy as a loon, and scary as a roaring lion. ("Legion" means "a lot." A Roman legion could be several thousand soldiers.) Jesus walks straight up to him and tells the spirits to take a flying leap into a lake. And they do (Mark 5:1-13).

Some miracles reveal his power over our worst enemy—death. Asked by a desperate father to save his dying daughter, Jesus arrives at the man's home too late. The little girl is dead. But Jesus walks into the dead girl's room, takes her by the hand, and says, "Little girl, get up!" She does. Everyone is astonished. Wouldn't you be? (See Mark 5:35-43.)

Jesus's Teachings

People flock to Jesus because the things that come out of his mouth are amazing. He doesn't give lists of dos and don'ts—he describes who God is and what life in his Kingdom is like.

Sometimes Jesus gives crystal-clear moral lessons, like "Do to others whatever you would like them to do to you" (Matthew 7:12). This lesson, which we call the Golden Rule, is what God wants all human relationships to look like. But Jesus knows that life is more than rules. He tells colorful and memorable stories that the average kid in his day can understand. These stories, called parables, reveal the true nature of God.

Three of his most famous parables are found in Luke 15.

In the first story, a sheep strays from its flock and gets lost. Its shepherd leaves ninety-nine safe sheep to find it. When he finds the lost sheep, the shepherd throws a party (Luke 15:1-7).

In the second story, a valuable coin slips from a woman's hand and rolls away. It's lost. She turns her house upside down, looking for the coin until she finds it. Then she invites friends and neighbors over for a celebration (Luke 15:8-10).

The third story is about a father and his two sons. The youngest son, sick of playing by the rules, leaves home with his share of the family money. He spends it like crazy and ends up broke. He decides to go home and apologize. He will ask to be a servant since he knows he doesn't deserve to be called a son.

When he goes home, to his complete surprise, the father receives him with love and mercy. The father throws a party that is heard for miles around. (Have you noticed the party pattern yet?)

When the older son hears that his reckless brother has returned home to a hero's welcome, he blows a gasket. Why does the kid who breaks all the rules get a party, but the son who obeys all the rules gets nothing? His father explains, "Look, dear son, you have always stayed by me, and everything I have is yours. We had to celebrate this happy day. Your brother was dead and has come back to life! He was lost, but now he is found!" (Luke 15:11-32).

In each of these stories, we learn that God, the Father of Jesus, cares deeply about anyone who is lost.

Jesus's Friendships

Finally, the people love Jesus because he offers them his friendship. When it comes to choosing friends, Jesus includes everyone, everywhere.

- Whom does he choose for his twelve disciples, his closest friends? A hotheaded zealot, a hated tax collector, and some smelly fishermen. Talk about diversity!

- When he encounters people caught in sin, what does he do? Forgives them.

- When he meets despised neighbors who are considered "sinners," how does he treat them? He has dinner with them. He doesn't mind being called a "friend of sinners."

Jesus accepts everyone, even (maybe especially) those who are thought to be far from God.

Rejection

But not everyone likes his miracles. After Jesus raises his good friend Lazarus from the dead, the Pharisees and Sadducees become afraid. A man who can raise the dead can also raise an army. They fear Jesus will try to lead a rebellion against Rome, and Rome will destroy Jerusalem in retaliation.

Not everyone likes his teachings either. When Jesus claims to have authority and power to forgive sins, the Pharisees and Sadducees accuse him of blasphemy (the worst possible sin).

And definitely not everyone likes his choice of friends. Every time he shares a meal with "sinners," it's a brand-new scandal for the religious leaders to hold against him.

For these reasons, the religious leaders decide that Jesus must die.

During the last six months of his life, Jesus knows he has made enemies among people in power. He knows their plans, yet he trusts God for his future. So in the spring of 30 AD, he heads to Jerusalem for the final showdown.

His Last Week

Each day of his final week is significant.

On Sunday, he enters the capital city on a donkey, with crowds singing and shouting, "Hosanna to the Son of David," meaning "You're our king! You're our new David! You're the one who can save us from our enemies!"

> The account of Jesus's last week takes up from 25 to 50 percent of each of the four Gospels. That shows how crucial his final days were to his story.

On Monday he heads for the Temple, where he confronts merchants gouging worshippers by selling sacrificial animals at sky-high prices. He tells them, "The Scriptures declare, 'My Temple will be called a house of prayer,' but you have turned it into a den of thieves!" (Matthew 21:13). He overturns their sales booths and drives everybody out.

On Tuesday he teaches in the Temple courtyards. The religious leaders try to play a game of Stump the Rabbi. He answers all their tough questions, asks them tougher questions, and mops the floor with them. He calls out the experts in the law of Moses for their hypocrisy—saying one thing and doing another. They do not take it well.

We don't know what Jesus does on Wednesday. We assume he has a quiet rest with his friends.

On Thursday Jesus hosts a Passover meal for his disciples. He ends the meal by telling the twelve that he is about to die on their behalf. He leads his inner circle into a nearby olive grove to pray. As the night gets darker, one disciple betrays Jesus to his enemies. They arrest him and lead him off to be tried. He is beaten and mocked all along the way.

On Friday, the Roman governor, Pilate, indicts Jesus on the accusation of claiming to be the king of the Jews, a crime punishable by death on a cross. Roman soldiers lead Jesus to a hill outside the city that looks like a skull, where they crucify him. They nail him to a cross at nine in the morning, where he hangs for six hours, mostly silent. But the few words he speaks reveal who he really is.

His Last Words

Here are Jesus's seven statements from the cross.

- "Father, forgive them, for they don't know what they are doing" (Luke 23:34).

- "I assure you, today you will be with me in paradise" (Luke 23:43).

- "When Jesus saw his mother standing there beside the disciple he loved, he said to her, 'Dear woman, here is your son.' And he said to this disciple, 'Here is your mother.' And from then on this disciple took her into his home" (John 19:26-27).

- "'*Eloi, Eloi, lema sabachthani?*' which means 'My God, my God, why have you abandoned me?'" (Mark 15:34).

- "Jesus knew that his mission was now finished, and to fulfill Scripture he said, 'I am thirsty'" (John 19:28).

- "Jesus said, 'It is finished!'" (John 19:30).

- "Then Jesus shouted, 'Father, I entrust my spirit into your hands!' And with those words he breathed his last" (Luke 23:46).

Jesus is dead. He is buried in a borrowed grave on a Friday afternoon right before the Sabbath begins.

But the story is not over!

On Sunday morning, God raises Jesus back to life! We call it the resurrection. It shows that love is stronger than evil. It proves once and for all that God is love and that Jesus is his Son.

That's the Jesus story.

How does your story fit into the Jesus story? First, he gave you a pattern to follow. Jesus was divine but also human. Like all humans—like you—he had to deal with being anonymous, being popular, and being rejected. Here's what we can learn from him as we face each experience.

 FACING ANONYMITY

Everyone wants to feel important. It's only natural that when you feel unnoticed and unknown, you also wind up feeling lost and lonely. When you feel this way, don't lash out in anger or give up. Instead, do these two things: First, ask God to help you meet someone who can become a friend. Having one good friend can make all the difference.

Second, draw close to God. Set aside a time and place to be alone with God. Be honest with him. Don't just say what you think you're supposed to say. He knows what you're thinking and how you're feeling, so you won't surprise him. God knows you. That can truly be enough.

FACING POPULARITY

Let's face it—being popular is fun. But popularity has a dark side. It can turn us into people pleasers. Soon, every move we make is just to get more "likes" on social media or in real life.

Remember how Jesus handled his popularity—he lived his life before an audience of One. You can make the same choice. Seek God's approval. If others clap for you, that's fine. But beware of crowds. They can crown you or crucify you, and they often don't care which.

FACING REJECTION

Nobody handles rejection better than Jesus. He doesn't defend himself against his enemies, and he doesn't retaliate. He relies on his heavenly Father and knows that the Father's love will see him through. Faith in God gives him the strength to take each step, especially during his final week. He knows enough about God to know that resurrection follows death.

Following Jesus means living for him and living like him. When we face rejection, we do what Jesus has done. We tell God what we are feeling, we ask for what we hope he will do, and then we release our control over the outcome, saying, "Yet I want your will to be done, not mine" (Matthew 26:39).

We trust that God can transform death into new life. This is how we face rejection and are not defeated.

JESUS HAS COME TO SAVE YOU

"God Saves" is the title of this chapter. Here is what it means to you personally.

First, God created you. Your father and mother certainly played a big role, but behind it all is God. He is your Maker. He wants you to exist.

Second, God knows you. He knows the good and rejoices in it. He knows the bad and the ugly, and he wants to help you work through them. He sees all of you, your whole self.

Third, God loves you, just as you are. Not only that, he likes you too! The minister and children's television pioneer Mister Rogers captures God's attitude toward you in a song:

> It's you I like,
> It's not the things you wear,
> It's not the way you do your hair
> But it's you I like
> The way you are right now,
> The way down deep inside you

Not the things that hide you,
Not your toys
They're just beside you.
But it's you I like
Every part of you.
Your skin, your eyes, your feelings
Whether old or new.
I hope that you'll remember
Even when you're feeling blue
That it's you I like.
It's you yourself.
It's you.
It's you I like.*

Fourth, God wants to save you. Why? So that you can experience his love today. So that you can live with him and enjoy him both now and forever.

Fifth, God loves you so much that he sent his Son, Jesus, to be born for you. To live for you. To die for you. To be raised for you. He sent Jesus to save you.

How exactly does Jesus save you?

He saves you by taking your place. Because of our sin, we all deserve death. But because Jesus, who lived a perfect life, died in our place, we are forgiven. When we trust in his forgiveness, we are saved from the

---

guilt of our sin and are free to live the very best life Jesus has planned for us in this life and the next.

Jesus saves! Hallelujah! (Which means, God be praised!)

The Story Between the Story

Jesus is alive, death is defeated, and it's time for the victory tour! Jesus appears to the women at his tomb, then to his disciples, and then to lots of other people—there is even a time when he appears to more than five hundred at once. A bunch of people see the risen Jesus with their own eyes, which is a big reason the Gospel doesn't die out after Jesus's very public crucifixion. Jesus is back, and the disciples are pumped! But after forty days, he tells them the Holy Spirit is coming to help them, and he then goes up to heaven right before their eyes.

Not long after this, the disciples are gathered together in Jerusalem when a rushing wind blows through the room. It's the Holy Spirit filling each of them with himself...and with the ability to speak a different language. This comes in handy when they go outside and find a crowd made up of Jews from all over the world who—you guessed it—speak a bunch of different languages. Peter preaches, Jews from all over the world are saved, and three thousand new believers are baptized (and they only counted the men)!

The church in Judea and Samaria grows like nobody's business, and the Pharisees are none too pleased. One of them, Saul, is a real go-getter, determined to stop these crazy Jesus-followers even if it means killing them. He gets permission to take a road trip to Damascus and drag any believers he finds back to Jerusalem in chains. On the road, a blinding light stops Saul in his tracks, and a voice asks, "Saul, why are you persecuting me?" It's Jesus (awkward!), and Saul doesn't really have a good answer for him. After a personal encounter with the risen Jesus and a three-day time-out in Damascus, Saul's sight is restored and he switches sides, becoming the ultimate go-getter for the Gospel. After meeting Jesus, he's a completely different person. He even starts going by his Greek name, Paul.

And that, in a nutshell, is the story between the story.

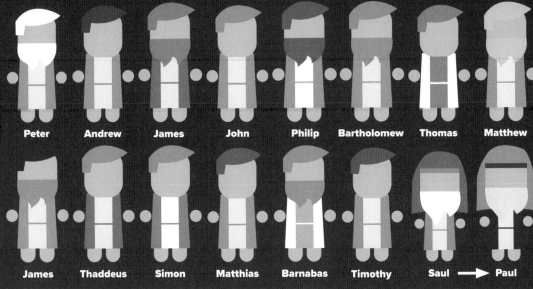

Peter, Andrew, James, John, Philip, Bartholomew, Thomas, Matthew

James, Thaddeus, Simon, Matthias, Barnabas, Timothy, Saul → Paul

Pharisees

Jesus

THE HOLY SPIRIT IS COMING TO HELP

I'LL BE BACK

7

God Sends

After Jesus's crucifixion and resurrection, Jesus's followers spread his story all over the city of Jerusalem, the region of Judea, and even to not-so-friendly nearby Samaria.

But for the Gospel to travel to the ends of the earth, God needs someone very special for the job. So he chooses…Saul of Tarsus? Wait, this can't be right. Saul? The fanatic who hates Christians? The man on a personal mission to arrest anyone connected to Christ and rid Judaism of those who call Jesus the Messiah? *That* Saul?

We've seen God pick some unlikely characters to play a part in his Great Story, but this takes the cake. For whatever mysterious reason, God wants to send Saul. So God surprises him by showing up in a big way while he is on a road trip to persecute more of Jesus's followers. (More on this later, but for now, let's just say Saul has a big-time change of heart!)

After his conversion, Saul starts going by his Greek name, Paul. He learns all he can about Jesus. He studies and prays in the desert. He reads the Hebrew Scriptures, searching for promises about the Messiah. One day he gets a message straight from God: He and his mentor, Barnabas, are to be the first missionaries.

They travel northwest until they come to the area that today we call Turkey. Their message gets mixed reviews. Some love it, some hate it (and say so with clubs and sticks), and some are on the fence. After months on the road and more than a few rejections and beatings, they return to Antioch to report to the church there.

Paul heads out again for parts unknown, this time with a new partner named Silas. Halfway into the trip, God sends them to Europe. They plant churches in major hubs like Philippi, Athens, and Corinth. On the way home, Paul stops in Ephesus and starts a new church there. Once again the reception is mixed—some believe the message, some don't, and some decide to make trouble.

Paul returns to Jerusalem, knowing he will face big trouble. He is arrested and put on trial for his life. His case ends up going all the way to the courts in Rome. All along the way, from Judea, to Caesarea, to Rome itself, Paul defends his faith, tells the Jesus story, and invites everyone to believe. Those who believe Paul spread the Good News of Jesus everywhere. The Gospel reaches the ends of the earth through the work of Paul, a most unlikely choice.

Jesus is the climax of God's Great Story. His life, death, and resurrection are Good News for the whole world. But only a handful of people in a tiny corner of the world know about it at first. How does the message spread to the whole world?

JESUS'S MARCHING ORDERS

Before Jesus goes back to heaven, he gives marching orders to his followers:

> You will receive power when the Holy Spirit comes upon you. And you will be my witnesses, telling people about me everywhere—in Jerusalem, throughout Judea, in Samaria, and to the ends of the earth (Acts 1:8).

The book of Acts records how the first Christians fulfill this command, first in Jerusalem, then in Judea and Samaria, and then to the ends of the earth.

Fifty days after Jesus's resurrection, Simon Peter tells the Jesus story to a huge crowd in Jerusalem at the Feast of Pentecost. Three thousand believe the story! Their lives are changed, and they are baptized to show their friends and families that they are now following Jesus. It's an amazing start, but things soon get rocky for Peter. He and John are arrested, beaten, and ordered to keep quiet. They don't listen. They keep telling the Good News in Jerusalem, and the word spreads.

A few years later, Stephen tells the Jesus story to a packed-out synagogue in Jerusalem and is quickly stoned to death by the crowd. Facing a similar fate, many Jesus-followers in the city head for the hills of Judea and Samaria.

In Samaria, Philip tells some locals about Jesus, and they believe. He then tells the Jesus story to a North African court official who also believes and is baptized. Soon Peter takes a big leap and tells Cornelius, a Roman military officer and godly Gentile, that he too can be saved through Christ even though he isn't a Jew. And Cornelius is saved along with his whole household. The Good News in Judea? Check. Samaria? Check. There's just one more step, and it's a big one.

Enter Saul of Tarsus, whom we know as Paul the apostle.

FROM SAUL OF TARSUS TO PAUL THE APOSTLE

Over half of the book of Acts is about Paul. Other than Jesus, he is the most influential and important person in the New Testament. His story is told in three key parts.

Saul Without Jesus

Saul is born in the Roman city of Tarsus about the same time Jesus is born in the Jewish city of Bethlehem. Saul becomes a Pharisee like his father before him. When a group of Jews start saying Jesus is Lord and Messiah, he does everything in his power to destroy them.

Before Saul meets Jesus, here is how Luke (the author of Acts) introduces him:

> The Jewish leaders were infuriated by Stephen's accusation, and they shook their fists at him in rage...They rushed at him and dragged him out of the city and began to stone him. His accusers took off their coats and laid them at the feet of a young man named Saul.
>
> They stoned [Stephen]...and with that, he died.
>
> Saul was one of the witnesses, and he agreed completely with the killing of Stephen (Acts 7:54-8:1).

Later, Saul himself admits his part in the persecution.

> You have heard of my previous way of life in Judaism, how intensely I persecuted the church of God and tried to destroy it (Galatians 1:13 NIV).

Early on, Saul believes God wants him to destroy the church. But his whole life soon turns upside down.

Saul Meets Jesus

Saul's story of meeting Jesus is a big deal. The book of Acts tells it three times to make sure you don't miss it. Here are the highlights (paraphrased from Acts 9:1-15).

Saul is a one-man wrecking machine. His goal? To wipe out the story that Jesus is the Messiah.

His plan? To arrest followers of the Way. (This is what the earliest followers of Jesus are called because they followed Jesus's way of life—makes sense, doesn't it?) Then to bring them to Jerusalem to face the Jewish Sanhedrin, where they must deny Jesus or die.

One day while traveling to Damascus to arrest Jesus-followers, Saul is struck down by a heavenly light. Lying in the dirt, he hears a voice thundering, "Saul! Why are you hunting and harassing me?"

Clueless, Saul asks, "Who's talking to me?"

The voice answers, "I am Jesus. I'm the one you're mistreating. Now go on into Damascus and wait for me to contact you."

Blinded by the light, Saul is led into Damascus and waits for three days. God finally sends Ananias, a Jesus-follower, to Saul with a message: "God has chosen you to take the Jesus story far and wide—to Jews whom you love and to non-Jews whom you don't love. And along the way, you will suffer more than you can imagine." (This last part sounds a bit scary, but Saul is willing to trust that Jesus knows what he is doing!)

This is the turning point for Saul. From now on, he is God's man through and through.

Paul with Jesus

After meeting Jesus on the Damascus Road, Saul goes into the desert to study Scripture...for ten years. That sounds like a long time to prepare for just about anything, but God has given Saul a really important job, and he wants him to be ready!

After Saul's decade in the desert, God gives the church in Antioch an assignment to send Saul and Barnabas out into the world.

> Among the prophets and teachers of the church at Antioch of Syria were Barnabas, Simeon...Lucius...Manaen...and Saul. One day as these men were worshiping the Lord and fasting, the Holy Spirit said, "Appoint Barnabas and Saul for the special work to which I have called them." So after more fasting and prayer, the men laid their hands on them and sent them on their way. So Barnabas and Saul were sent out by the Holy Spirit (Acts 13:1-4).

Saul's role as Jesus's ambassador to the world is official! Over the next several years he leads three massive mission trips, taking the Gospel message to the known world.

First Mission Trip (See Acts 13–14)

Saul (now known as Paul) takes two companions along on his first trip—Barnabas and Mark. Barnabas is the key leader at the church in Antioch, and Mark is Barnabas's younger cousin. They set out for Cyprus, where Barnabas is from, and then head north to Galatia (in modern-day Turkey).

They start by telling the Jesus story to Jews in the synagogue. If the Jews receive the message, great. If not, they go to plan B—telling Jesus's story to the Gentiles. Even though there is a lot of suffering along the way (Paul gets stoned almost to death at one point), his trip is a success. Paul starts several new churches, and many Jews and non-Jews alike turn to Christ.

Second Mission Trip (See Acts 16–18)

Paul takes two new partners, Silas and Timothy, on his second mission trip.

After visiting the churches that were planted on the first trip, they travel to major cities in Greece and stay in each one as long as they can. But people are still angry at Paul from his first trip. Not surprisingly, in almost every city he enters, he is either arrested or kicked out.

He manages to stay eighteen months in Corinth. He also writes letters to several of the churches he has planted. And once more, many people come to faith in Jesus, and many new churches are started.

Third Mission Trip (See Acts 19–21)

Paul takes his third and final mission trip in the mid-50s AD, visiting the churches he planted earlier, before settling down in Ephesus for two years. He writes more letters to churches, not knowing that his words one day will become part of the church's Scripture.

Arrest, Trial, and Release

After escaping a huge riot in Ephesus, God gives Paul a surprising vision: Paul must go to Jerusalem.

Wait, Jerusalem? The place where they crucified Jesus? And stoned Stephen to death? *That* Jerusalem? Yep. But Paul is not afraid.

> And now I am bound by the Spirit to go to Jerusalem. I don't know what awaits me, except that the Holy Spirit tells me in city after city that jail and suffering lie ahead. But my life is worth nothing to me unless I use it for finishing the work assigned me by the Lord Jesus—the work of telling others the Good News about the wonderful grace of God (Acts 20:22-24).

So Paul sails to Jerusalem. He's been in town less than a week when an angry mob drags him out of the Temple and throws him in jail. Paul goes to court. He tells about his conversion to Christ. Another riot ensues. Paul is thrown back in jail. Not again!

Forty assassins make an oath to kill Paul before they eat another meal, which sounds a little extreme, don't you think? Thankfully, a Roman officer at the jail hears about their plan and smuggles Paul out of Jerusalem in the middle of the night, taking him to Caesarea and leaving the forty assassins incredibly hangry.

In Caesarea, Paul is locked away in prison for two years. He argues his case before two Roman high officials. They decide that Paul has not broken any Roman laws, so they try to send him back to the Jewish court in Jerusalem. Paul refuses. Going back to Jerusalem means death for sure. So Paul claims his right as a Roman citizen to have a trial before the Roman emperor himself.

In the fall of 60 AD, Paul sails to Rome as a prisoner awaiting trial before Emperor Nero. After two years of waiting, he wins his trial and is released.

For five more years, Paul tries to travel west to Spain, but we don't know if he ever makes it that far.

Finally, Paul is arrested for the last time. He goes on trial in Rome again, and this time he is found guilty. According to tradition, he is executed outside of Rome in the mid-60s.

So ends the life of the most influential Christian and missionary in the history of the church. But here is a question you need to ask yourself as you think about Paul and the way he lived...

Like Saul or like Paul?

Some people try to make everything about themselves look perfect on the outside, even though on the inside they are hurting, or doubting, or falling to pieces. They rely on their own ability to follow rules to the letter. They don't think they need God's grace or that he will help them unless they behave perfectly.

But there are others who know they don't have it all together. They dare to believe that Jesus's grace can heal them and change their lives. They throw themselves on his grace and are transformed.

Saul of Tarsus belongs in the first group. Paul the apostle belongs in the second.

Are you more like Saul or more like Paul?

No Comparison

Paul writes in a letter from jail about how Jesus has changed everything in his life. He compares his life without Christ to his life with Christ. Can you see the dramatic difference between the two?

> I was circumcised when I was eight days old. I am a pure-blooded citizen of Israel and a member of the tribe of Benjamin—a real Hebrew if there ever was one! I was a member of the Pharisees, who demand the strictest obedience to the Jewish law. I was so zealous that I harshly persecuted the church. And as for righteousness, I obeyed the law without fault.

> I once thought these things were valuable, but now I consider them worthless because of what Christ has done. Yes, everything else is worthless when compared with the infinite value of knowing Christ Jesus my Lord. For his sake I have discarded everything else, counting it all as garbage, so that I could gain Christ...I want to know Christ and experience the mighty power that raised him from the dead. I want to suffer with him, sharing in his death, so that one way or another I will experience the resurrection from the dead!...

> I focus on this one thing: Forgetting the past and looking forward to what lies ahead, I press on to reach the end of the

race and receive the heavenly prize for which God, through Christ Jesus, is calling us (Philippians 3:5-14).

Paul says incredible things about his transformation in Christ. They could be paraphrased like this:

- "My old life is pointless when I compare it to Jesus's sacrifice for me."

- "My old life is worthless compared to the treasure of knowing Jesus firsthand."

- "I am now so single-minded that all I want in life is to know Jesus."

Transformation like this doesn't happen all at once; it takes a lifetime to learn this new way of life. What's important is not how perfect you are. What matters is this: What direction are you facing? Who are you becoming? What do you love most in life?

Reflecting on Paul's story, you can't help but see three surprises.

GOD CHOOSES SURPRISING PEOPLE

Saul of Tarsus is the last person you'd expect to tell the Good News of Jesus anywhere. He hates everything about the church. He believes that anyone who talks about Jesus as the Messiah is not only wrong but should also be killed. How incredible then that Paul is chosen to take the Jesus story all over the known world!

We see this happen time and time again in God's Great Story. From Abraham, to Moses, to David, God chooses the most unlikely people and uses them to accomplish his purpose in the world.

If God can choose such surprising people to do his work, God can definitely choose you!

GOD SENDS PEOPLE TO SURPRISING PLACES

Have you read *Oh, the Places You'll Go!* by Dr. Seuss? It talks about all the surprising sites you may one day see. But even Dr. Seuss might be surprised to discover the unexpected places God sends those who are ready to serve him.

I (Paul) have a relative named Chris Harmon. Chris is a dermatologist—a medical doctor who helps heal people's skin. One day God called Chris and his wife, Sandy, to use Chris's medical skills far from his comfortable home in the United States. Chris and Sandy went on medical mission trips to Venezuela and Bolivia, serving the poorest of the poor. Then they sensed God calling them to do the same along the Amazon River in Brazil. They went on to serve in many other countries as ambassadors of Jesus. They never dreamed they would go so many places in their lifetime, but God had different plans.

God loves to send people to surprising places. If God can send Chris and Sandy Harmon throughout South America, God can send you.

GOD USES PEOPLE TO DO SURPRISINGLY GREAT THINGS

It's easy to forget that even the most extraordinary people start off in ordinary ways. They had ordinary childhoods, often ordinary adulthoods, before they ever did anything considered great. Consider these examples.

Mother Teresa

Mother Teresa was born Mary Teresa Bojaxhiu, an unknown girl from a tiny European country. She taught school in India for seventeen years. Then one day she felt called by God to serve people living in extreme poverty on the streets of Calcutta, India. After years of difficult, exhausting work, she won the Nobel Peace Prize in 1979. This little Albanian nun organized thousands of people to serve millions of the sick and poor in the name of Christ. She did something surprisingly great for God.

Francis Collins

Born in rural Virginia and growing up on a small farm raising cows and sheep, Francis Collins probably wasn't expected to do great things. But when he discovered a passion to help others through the study of genetics, he began to shine. He studied for years and got both a PhD (meaning he's an expert thinker) and an MD (meaning he's an expert healer). He became the director of the National Institutes for Health. He led the Human Genome Project, which identified the gene for cystic fibrosis, giving scientists a better chance to understand and cure this terrible disease. Along the way he gave his life to Jesus Christ as his Lord and Savior, dedicating all his healing work to the glory of God. He is doing something surprisingly great for God.

Dallas Willard

You wouldn't think a college professor could help change the world, but Dallas Willard did just that. Young Dallas had a really hard start. His mother died when he was a child. He never had a steady home growing up. He was passed around from family member to family member until he went off to college to become a teacher. He was fascinated with the world of philosophy, so he got a PhD in it. He ended up teaching philosophy at the University of Southern California for forty-seven years.

After a while, he was asked to preach and teach Bible studies in churches near where he lived, so he did. He didn't know it then, but those lessons he taught would one day become modern classics. His books have impacted countless lives by teaching about the nature and love of God. Dallas loved God, loved teaching students, and loved making discipleship accessible to anyone. He did something surprisingly great for God.

 ## ARE YOU READY TO BE SENT?

Just because Jesus is the climax of God's Great Story doesn't mean the story is over.

For two thousand years now, Christians have been living in the time of *sending*. This is the time when God's Spirit is sending out his people to tell the Jesus story in all parts of the world.

You are alive during this time of sending.

Are you ready to be sent?

The Story Between the Story

The early church spreads like wildfire, thanks to the blessing of the Holy Spirit. God sends the apostles to preach the Gospel throughout the known world, and they also write some very important letters. These letters help encourage followers of Jesus, instruct them in truth, and correct false teaching. And what's really cool is that those same letters continue to speak to all of us today through the New Testament.

Unfortunately, not everybody is stoked to hear the good news of Jesus, and the apostles also have to put up with some heavy persecution. It seems wherever they carry news about Jesus, they encounter both blessing (as some people receive the Gospel) and opposition (as others reject it). The Roman emperor at this time, Nero, is a seriously bad dude who basically kills Christians for fun. And one of his successors, Domitian, isn't much of an improvement. Along with lots of other Christians, the apostles are tortured and eventually killed for their testimony about the risen Jesus. One by one, all of them are martyred. That is, all except one. The apostle John, the beloved disciple who had been one of the original twelve, is tortured by Domitian and then exiled to the Island of Patmos.

It is a very difficult time for followers of Jesus to hold on to their faith. But just as they begin to feel that they are being overwhelmed by persecution, God sends them some special encouragement through John and his visionary letter called Revelation, telling them to hang on because God is going to win in the end!

And that, in a nutshell, is the story between the story.

Nero   **Domitian**

The Apostles

Island of Patmos

Hang on because God is going to win in the end!

8

God Wins

As long as we humans have lived on this earth, we have told so many stories. There are too many to count! The stories that last, that get retold again and again, have one thing in common—a good ending. Have you ever sat through a super long movie and when the ending finally played, it was terrible? "You're kidding me! That's it?" you might yell at the screen. All that time and energy spent following a story, and suddenly the movie ends with a black screen and an empty feeling.

What makes a bad ending? Sometimes the storyteller ends by trying to explain everything you already know from the story. It's kind of like telling a bad joke: If you have to explain it, it's usually not very funny. Same with a story—if it has to be explained, it means the storyteller didn't do a very good job telling it.

Sometimes it feels like the writer just runs out of steam and slaps together a lame ending, hoping no one will notice. We notice. (And we hate it.)

Some endings are just plain confusing. When the credits roll you scratch your head and go, "Uh, what just happened?"

So, what makes for a good ending? Most good stories have one or both of these two things: resolution and redemption.

Resolution means all the loose ends are tied up. A mystery is solved. Quests are accomplished. Relationships are restored. Sam Gamgee says it well in *The Return of the King*: "I shan't call it the end, till we've cleared up the mess."

Redemption happens when something is learned, something of great value is gained, or someone is changed. In the Disney hit *Frozen*, Anna saves Elsa's life by putting herself between Elsa and certain death. This act of true love transforms Elsa into the person she was meant to be. Elsa's redemption through her sister's brave act is what makes the ending so good. (Making sure Olaf the snowman doesn't melt also really helps.)

A story doesn't *have* to have both resolution and redemption to end well. The best endings, though, have both.

Take the classic story of *Les Misérables*. (It's a book! It's a movie! It's a big giant musical! Check it out!) In *Les Misérables*, Jean Valjean is a criminal on the run who is shown grace by a Catholic priest. It changes his life. At the end of the story, Valjean is an old man surrounded by people who have experienced grace because of him. He is led into heaven by the bishop who first showed him kindness, and by Fantine, the first person he showed grace to, as they all sing a moving chorus that resolves the story.

It's a powerful ending.

Which brings us to the end of God's Great Story. You've read how God creates, blesses, rescues, chooses, warns, saves, and sends his people.

And now, the big finish—God wins!

It's the ultimate resolution, and redemption has the final word.

In the end, God wins, and it changes everything!

 GOD WINS IN THE END

In three of the four Gospels, Jesus reveals to his disciples the biggest spoiler alert ever: One day he will return and tie up all the loose ends of history (Matthew 24; Mark 13; Luke 21:5-36). The apostle Paul tells us that in a moment, in the blink of an eye, the trumpet will sound and the end will come (1 Corinthians 15:52). But the big preview of the final act is the Revelation of John, written near the end of the first century AD. And it is a doozy.

Revelation is epic. It has everything: battles, earthquakes, plagues, scary horsemen, and even a fiery dragon. And just when it seems like all is lost, a sudden turn of events gives hope to the hopeless. It is a glimpse of the final victory!

A Come-from-Behind Victory

The Roman emperor Nero is a bad, bad man. He puts Peter and Paul to death. He uses Christians as human streetlights by sticking them on posts and lighting them on fire.

Domitian, who rules Rome from 90 to 95 AD, kills members of his own family whom he suspects of following Jesus. John, the last living disciple of the original twelve, is persecuted by Domitian and exiled to Patmos. Times are tough!

Roman emperors demand that people bow down to them as their lord. Christianity's devotion to the lordship of Christ means they can't do that. It is a big problem. Many believers refuse to bow to the Caesar and declare that Jesus is Lord. It does not go well for them in this life.

John can't talk openly about the bad things happening to his fellow Christians, so he writes about them using dramatic symbols that his intended readers will immediately understand. It gets pretty wild. There are dragons and beasts and angels with lion heads...all sorts of vivid images that help Christians recognize his message: It's tough now, and things don't look good, but hold on because God will win in the end!

An Unlikely Hero

John goes into heaven in a vision. There he sees a throne surrounded by twenty-four elders, representing the people of God from both Testaments (twelve tribes of Israel + twelve disciples of Jesus = twenty-four elders in heaven). The Lord sits on the throne. In his right hand, he's holding a scroll that is closed with a seal that no one in the room can open. John tells what happens next:

> Then I began to weep bitterly because no one was found worthy to open the scroll and read it. But one of the twenty-four elders said to me, "Stop weeping! Look, the Lion of the tribe of Judah, the heir to David's throne, has won the victory. He is worthy to open the scroll and its seven seals."

> Then I saw a Lamb that looked as if it had been slaughtered, but it was now standing between the throne and the four living beings and among the twenty-four elders…And when he took the scroll, the four living beings and the twenty-four elders fell down before the Lamb…And they sang a new song with these words:

> > "You are worthy to take the scroll
> >   and break its seals and open it.
> > For you were slaughtered, and your blood
> >   has ransomed people for God
> >   from every tribe and language and people and nation.

And you have caused them to become
 a Kingdom of priests for our God.
 And they will reign on the earth" (Revelation 5:4-6,8-9).

The Lion of Judah is a Lamb. An unlikely hero for sure. How does a Lamb defeat the powers of the evil one and his minions? Don't we need a big, powerful hero to knock out the devil with a mighty punch?

No! God knows that power can control evil, but it cannot get rid of it for good. Look around at human history...the violent use of power only creates seeds for more violence in the hearts of the victims, and those seeds always sprout again.

Jesus allows himself to be beaten, whipped, and nailed to the cross. Satan delivers every blow he can to defeat God's ultimate plan for saving and rescuing humanity. But love—perfect, sacrificial love—cannot be defeated by hatred, force, and violence. Jesus does not answer his accusers, or mock his executioners, or call down ten thousand angels to fight for him. Instead he calls out to his Father from the cross, "Forgive them, for they don't know what they are doing" (Luke 23:34).

In his effort to destroy Jesus, Satan uses up his last trick. He's out of gas. Totally exhausted. Practically all the Lord Almighty has to do is breathe on him, and Satan falls to his eternal demise.

The Score Is Settled

Over the centuries, Christianity has faced a huge question: What do we do with evil and suffering? Man's inhumanity to man seems limitless.

When bad things keep happening and nothing seems to get better, the only hope left is that one day God will set everything right. John's revelation voices this great hope for those who suffer at the hands of others:

> And I saw a great white throne and the one sitting on it. The earth and sky fled from his presence, but they found no place to hide. I saw the dead, both great and small, standing before God's throne. And the books were opened, including the Book of Life. And the dead were judged according to what they had done, as recorded in the books. The sea gave up its dead, and death and the grave gave up their dead. And all were judged according to their deeds. Then death and the grave were thrown into the lake of fire. This lake of fire is the second death. And anyone whose name was not found recorded in the Book of Life was thrown into the lake of fire (Revelation 20:11-15).

The book recording all the hatred, betrayal, injustice, and unspeakable deeds done by everyone who has ever lived will be opened. Think about it like this: Everyone's life story is going to be posted on an eternal Facebook account. Everything will be exposed, and everything will be made right. The Lord of creation will hold everyone accountable for their actions.

Justice and judgment will come to everyone except those whose names are written in the Book of Life. On the cross, Christ has taken on the guilt and judgment of all people. But only those who have trusted in Christ will have their names written in that good book. Those whose names appear in the Book of Life will be spared from judgment and will live in the presence of God forever!

It Includes a Mind-Blowing Party!

The apostle Paul puts it as simply as he can: "No eye has seen, no ear has heard, and no mind has imagined what God has prepared for those who love him" (1 Corinthians 2:9).

Words alone don't come close to describing how glorious and jaw-dropping the celebration of God's win will be. Still, John paints a wondrous word picture using the imagery of a wedding.

> Then I heard again what sounded like the shout of a vast crowd
> or the roar of mighty ocean waves or the crash of loud thunder:
>
> "Praise the LORD!
>   For the Lord our God, the Almighty, reigns.
> Let us be glad and rejoice,
>   and let us give honor to him.
> For the time has come for the wedding feast of
> the Lamb,
>   and his bride has prepared herself"
>   (Revelation 19:6-7).

Jesus is the groom. His church (those who trust him) are his bride. The ceremony is now over. It's time to cut the cake and hit the dance floor! Eating and drinking, feasting and dancing, storytelling and remembering will go on for days! And everyone who says yes to Jesus, to his invitation, will make the guest list. If this sounds like your kind of party, the invitation is still open. The final verses of Revelation send out this invite:

> The Spirit and the bride say, "Come." Let anyone who hears this say, "Come." Let anyone who is thirsty come. Let anyone who desires drink freely from the water of life (Revelation 22:17).

 ## AND IT CHANGES EVERYTHING

> And the one sitting on the throne said. "Look, I am making everything new!" (Revelation 21:5).

Creation Will Be Renewed

God's Great Story certainly involves us humans, but at the end of time, God has a much larger vision of what is going to be made new than most of us do. The apostle Paul drops a hint in his letter to the believers in Rome:

> For all creation is waiting eagerly for that future day when God will reveal who his children really are. Against its will, all creation was subjected to God's curse. But with eager hope, the creation looks forward to the day when it will join God's children in glorious freedom from death and decay (Romans 8:19-21).

John's revelation picks up the trail:

> Then I saw a new heaven and a new earth, for the old heaven and the old earth had disappeared. And the sea was also gone.

> And I saw the holy city, the new Jerusalem, coming down
> from God out of heaven like a bride beautifully dressed for
> her husband (Revelation 21:1-2).

We aren't going to be whisked away to some amusement park in the sky, like an Outer Space Disneyland, by the way. Heaven and earth are going to be made new, right here where we are. Oceans and rivers will be crystal clear, skies will be brilliantly blue, the land will bear its fruit without hindrance, and God's creatures will nobly and peacefully roam the earth.

Reality Will Be Reordered

Isaiah (one of the prophets you met earlier) gives a sneak preview of the final chapter of God's Great Story. Spoiler alert: The story ends with all things being reordered, rearranged, and reimagined. Put another way, the world turns upside down. Here's a paraphrase of Isaiah's words:

> Armies will farm the land, not fight over it. Weapons, instruments of death, will be reshaped into tools for bringing life. Nations will make peace with each other. Their resources will be invested in the common good. Wolves will hang out with lambs, and no wool will fly. Leopards will curl up with baby goats for an afternoon nap. Hurt people will stop hurting other people. The earth will overflow with people who know and love God (see Isaiah 2:4; 11:6-9).

John's revelation echoes Isaiah's prophecy: "He will wipe every tear from their eyes. There will be no more death or mourning or crying or pain, for the old order of things has passed away" (Revelation 21:4 NIV).

Have you ever wondered what a new order of things might look like? Will time still exist? Will we be able to see God's presence 24/7? Will there still be gravity, or will we be able to fly effortlessly through the heavens and the earth? When it comes to relationships, will we know one another? Will everyone be best friends?

When we begin thinking about a new order of things, the questions are endless! But what matters is that whatever is broken now will be fixed for all time!

We Will Be Resurrected and Receive New Bodies

Being alive means that one day we all will get old, or sick, or hurt. And everyone, at some point, will die. But that isn't the final word on being alive! The apostle Paul tells us...

> It will happen in a moment, in the blink of an eye, when the last trumpet is blown. For when the trumpet sounds, those who have died will be raised to live forever. And we who are living will also be transformed. For our dying bodies must be transformed into bodies that will never die; our mortal bodies must be transformed into immortal bodies (1 Corinthians 15:52-53).

I (Jim) hold onto that hope myself. Not long before I was born, my father lost his leg in a terrible accident. He was an amazing dad, but there were a lot of things we couldn't do together. He couldn't run with me or go places really fast. I prayed that my dad could have both his legs again, but I would get upset when my prayers weren't answered.

My mom saw that I was having a hard time accepting my dad's condition. She told me about God's promise to make everything new. "One day, Jim," she told me, "when your dad is in heaven, he will have two good legs." I held on tight to this hope growing up. So did my dad. One day I asked him, "What are you going to do when you get to heaven?"

I'll never forget his answer: "I'm going to run and run till I can't run anymore."

We live inside frail, vulnerable, and mortal bodies. But in Jesus's resurrection and return, we have the hope of all hopes—a brand-new life and a new spiritual body made to last for all eternity. In the end, God wins—and so do we!

Knowing that God wins changes how we live here and now and forever. This is where your story comes in!

BECAUSE GOD WINS, WE CAN LIVE WITH CONFIDENCE

That's the purpose of Revelation. It is God's timeless reminder that he is in control. No matter what we face here and now, we can be confident because we know how things end!

You may be facing a difficult situation right this minute. You may not be doing well in school, or your parents might be getting a divorce. Someone might be bullying you. You might have had an argument with your friend or brother or sister and feel like you'll never be friends again. Someone you love may have moved away or even died.

Whatever is happening to you, don't panic or give up. These things do not decide who you are. These challenges cannot beat you or break you. In the end, everything gets resolved and redeemed. Because you know the ending, you can live right now with confidence and hope!

BECAUSE GOD WINS, WE CAN LIVE WITH PURPOSE

Near the end of Matthew's story of Jesus's life, he writes down three of Jesus's parables that talk about the end of the world as we know it. One of those parables is known today as the parable of the three servants (Matthew 25:14-30).

In this story, a master leaves on a long trip. Before he goes, he gives a lot of money to three servants for them to take care of while he is away. In the Bible, this kind of money is called a talent. One single talent is worth more than a million dollars!

The master gives one servant five talents, the next gets two talents, and the last servant gets one.

The master doesn't tell them what to do with the money. He just reminds them that he will come back for it someday. When he comes back, they have to tell him what they did with the wealth he gave them.

The first and second servants paid attention to their master, and now they put their knowledge to good use. Each of them doubles his money. The servant with two talents now has four! The servant with five talents now has ten!

The third servant is a different story. He is scared of messing up. Instead of doing what he has learned from the master, he buries his one talent in the ground so nothing can happen to it. And unfortunately for him, nothing does.

The master returns. The first two servants joyfully reveal how they have doubled the shares he gave them. The master then affirms and blesses them, saying, "Great job, guys! I trusted you with a relatively small responsibility—now I will give you even more! Let's go celebrate!"

Things don't go as well for the third servant. When the master sees that the servant hasn't done a single thing with his one talent, the master takes it away from him. The servant loses everything, and on top of that, he gets kicked out of the big party.

Don't miss the point! This parable gives a sneak preview of the future after God wraps everything up at Jesus's return. God promises two things. One promise is a big party! Awesome! Who doesn't love a big party? (If you don't, it's okay—the party is so big there's plenty of room to find a quiet spot.)

The other promise is something you might not expect. God promises us...more responsibility! Huh?

If you're worried that heaven is just one big long boring church service, Jesus has really good news for you! God wants us to help him be in charge of the new heavens and the new earth, just like he planned for us to do at the dawn of creation. (Remember that from chapter 1?)

This time, though, there will be no serpent in the garden. We will live and work along with God, living out new stories of his redeeming love. According to Jesus, eternity is going to be more active and purposeful than we can imagine.

It's hard to beat Dallas Willard's description of what lies in store for those who trust Jesus:

> Our destiny is to join a tremendously creative team effort, under unimaginably splendid leadership, on an inconceivably vast plane of activity, with ever more comprehensive cycles of productivity and enjoyment.*

Whatever you do, don't miss it! Live your one and only life in such a way that when the Master returns, you can hear him say to you, "Well done, my good and faithful servant. You have been faithful in handling this small amount, so now I will give you many more responsibilities. Let's celebrate together" (Matthew 25:21,23).

---

* Dallas Willard, *The Divine Conspiracy: Rediscovering Our Hidden Life in God* (San Francisco: Harper San Francisco, 1997), 399.

Finding Your Place

We hope our telling of God's Great Story has made you curious about God and what he is up to in our crazy world. We also hope we have helped you think about God more clearly. Even though we've come to the end of our book, this is not the end of God's story. As a matter of fact, we believe he is writing new chapters right now all over the world in the lives of *billions* of people who trust him. How cool is that!

And here's the really good news. God wants to include you. He has a special role for you in his story—a role that only you can play. Does that sound exciting? Does it sound scary? Does it sound like both? That's all okay! Some people are immediately stoked to hear that God has a special mission for them to accomplish with their life. But others hear the big news and respond just like Moses did when God called him:

"God, you can't mean me."

"I think you've got the wrong person."

"No one knows who I am."

"There must be someone who could do a better job than me."

If these thoughts are in your way, keeping you from finding your place in God's Great Story, I want to share with you one final thread that runs through every chapter you have just read. It is a secret message that will encourage you and bring you hope for a bright future. Here it is:

God surprises.

Here's what we mean. In every chapter, God chooses and uses people and circumstances that we normally wouldn't expect. He turns things upside down. He flips the script. He taps people on the shoulder—the "wrong" people, from a human perspective—and invites them to be the lead in a crucial part of the story. Check this out:

- An Almighty God could have created people as robots, programming them to do everything he wants all the time. Instead, he gives people, his special creation, the freedom to say yes or no to him, to follow him or turn their backs on him.

- God chose Abraham and Sarah, a childless couple way past childbearing age, to start a new tribe and nation of people.

- God called Moses to come out of retirement and lead God's people out of slavery in Egypt. Moses was way more comfortable watching sheep roam the desert than leading a million stubborn people through it.

- God picked David—the youngest son of Jesse, not the oldest—to be Israel's second king and forgave him when he made bad moral decisions that hurt himself and others.

- The prophets were a mixed bag of weird misfits whom God used to clarify his expectations and purposes for his people and to warn them to shape up or get ready to ship out.

- Jesus, God's Son and the King of kings, was not born in a palace of privilege but in a borrowed stable. He came to establish God's kingdom and rule on earth, but he didn't do it by the power of the sword, coercing people to follow him. Instead, he wooed people with the power of sacrificial love.

- Paul, the first missionary, was a super-spreader of the good news of Jesus. But before that, he tried to silence the message of Jesus by persecuting and killing those who were following him.

- And someday, even when most people will seem to be rejecting the message of Jesus and turning the world into one big dumpster fire, God will pull the biggest surprise of all by sending Jesus back to the earth to clean up the mess. Jesus will make all things right and all things new.

Do you feel the puzzle pieces clicking together? God's whole deal is not using people who have Marvel-like superpowers. Instead, he finds ordinary people who are more likely to have super flaws. How surprising is that?

Everyone—no matter how young or old, rich or poor; no matter where they live, how they look, or what they've done—*everyone* is invited to find their place in God's story. And that definitely includes you!

So, what will it be? Are you ready for an exciting new chapter in your life? Are you ready to follow Jesus wherever he leads you in your great story as you grow up, finish school, make friends, find a career path, start a family, and launch out into God's big, beautiful world? If you are, just whisper a prayer and let him know—then get ready to live out the great, challenging adventure that God has in store for you!

Acknowledgments

God's grace-gifts to us are many. Here are some we gratefully name:

Our family…

> Robin and Denise, thank you for being adventure-partners in life and in the Gospel as you have loved and lived out God's Great Story.

> Kari, Kristen, Ben, Tyler, and Brady, thank you for believing that the Story we told you when you were kids was worth giving your lives to as adults. It's fun watching you grow up.

Our collaborators…

> Tyler, thank you for your creativity and wit in every paragraph. You made this book better in every way.

> Allison, thank you for sharing your writing gift in The Story Between the Story. We look forward to reading your books one day.

Devon, thank you for pouring yourself into the graphics. They are as delightful as ever.

Our support team...

Gene, Kyle, Barb, and Bob at Harvest House Publishers, thank you for believing in this project before we did.

Keely, our agent at WordServe Literary, thank you for going the second mile time and again.

Our church family...

Preston Trail, thank you for supporting us in every good endeavor that God has called us to, including writing this book.

The boundary lines have indeed fallen for us in pleasant places (Psalm 16:6).

Jim and Paul

About the Authors

Paul Basden is a cofounding and senior pastor of Preston Trail Community Church in Frisco, Texas. A native of Dallas, Texas, Paul earned his BA from Baylor University and his Master of Divinity and PhD from Southwestern Theological Seminary. Paul also served as university minister and a professor of theology at Samford University in Birmingham, Alabama. He and his wife, Denise, have two grown daughters, a son-in-law, and four grandsons.

Jim Johnson is a cofounding and senior pastor of Preston Trail Community Church in Frisco, Texas. A native of Midland, Texas, Jim earned his Master of Divinity degree from Southwestern Theological Seminary and his BA and PhD from Baylor University. He and his wife, Robin, have three grown sons, a daughter-in-law, two granddaughters, and a grandson.